Case Study Analysis in the Classroom

Case Study Analysis in the Classroom

Becoming a Reflective Teacher

Renee Campoy

Murray State University

For information:

Sage Publications, Inc.
2455 Teller Road
Thousand Oaks, California 91320
E-mail: order@sagepub.com

Sage Publications Ltd.
1 Oliver's Yard
55 City Road
London EC1Y 1SP
United Kingdom

Sage Publications India Pvt. Ltd.
B-42, Panchsheel Enclave
Post Box 4109
New Delhi 110 017 India

Printed in the United States of America

Library of Congress Cataloging-in-Publication Data

Campoy, Renee W.
Case study analysis in the classroom: Becoming a reflective teacher / Renee Campoy.
p. cm.
Includes bibliographical references and index.
ISBN 0-7619-3028-0 (pbk.)
1. Reflective teaching. 2. Case method. I. Title.
LB1025.3.C35 2005
371.102—dc22 2004008077

This book is printed on acid-free paper.

04 05 06 07 10 9 8 7 6 5 4 3 2 1

Acquisitions Editor: Diane McDaniel
Editorial Assistant: Margo Crouppen
Production Editor: Denise Santoyo
Copy Editor: Mary L. Tederstrom
Typesetter: C&M Digitals (P) Ltd.
Indexer: Rachel Rice
Cover Designer: Janet Foulger

CONTENTS

ACKNOWLEDGMENTS

Many friends and colleagues assisted and inspired me in the writing of this book. Colleagues helped by providing insight and accuracy to improve case studies in their areas of expertise. These colleagues include Marty Dunham, Arlene Hall, Allison Hoewisch, Joy Navan, George Patmor, and Rich Radcliffe. In addition, Pam Miller was invaluable with her assistance in editing, providing content feedback, and, most of all, moral support.

HOW TO USE THIS BOOK

The activities in this book are based on my classroom experiences along with extensive investigation of how to help my own students become great teachers. For you, as a beginning teacher, the case studies will provide an analysis of and solutions for important and often controversial classroom situations. Such analysis promotes a reflective approach, where the teacher's classroom experiences, knowledge of content, and understanding of learning theory are considered during classroom problem solving. Ideally, all of us would prefer that these situations be experienced firsthand in schools. Unfortunately, this is often impossible to arrange. Impossible because the full array of educational experiences presented here may never occur. Impossible because experience has taught me that plans often go awry during field experiences. For example, even though my students may be placed in a highly diverse school, the actual students they work with may not be from a diverse population.

The conceptual framework of the book is constructivist learning theory. This perspective assumes that authentic learning and growth in understanding occur only when students are confronted with ideas that challenge existing assumptions and preconceived notions about education. The case studies are therefore necessarily challenging and controversial. Particularly the case studies in Chapter 2 are designed to expose you to situations that will reveal a need for new information and ways of looking at students and classrooms. This confrontation is not meant to be harsh or judgmental but to convince you of the need for change. You must change your thinking because teachers have special ways of thinking and solving problems that are different from how nonteachers think. As you review and analyze the case studies, you will revise your current thinking in order to begin to think and reflect like a teacher.

After the introduction in Chapter 1, Chapter 2 plunges you into the reflective problem-solving process. Each case study includes a rubric designed to stimulate your thinking and provide feedback about your reflective problem-solving skills. As your thinking changes from that of a nonteacher to a professional teacher, the rubrics in each case study provide feedback on your progress. The case study problems are complex and do not lend themselves to simple, straightforward answers. In fact, the objective of case study analysis is not to obtain the "right answer" according to the rubric but to increase your understanding of the situation. With this increased understanding, you will be better prepared to face similar situations in your own classroom.

Chapter 3 describes the process of reflective problem solving, and Chapter 4 provides the content used during the problem-solving process, including pedagogy, theory, and research. This is the content used for the philosophy of education that you will develop at the end of the chapter. Chapters 5 through 7 provide practice in reflective problem solving using a variety of case studies. These cases include some of the most difficult and often ignored issues by our society including topics of race, religion, and social class. The case studies vary in the level of controversy and challenge in terms of teacher experience and knowledge. Some are designed to address the concerns of a new teacher with little background and classroom experience, whereas others would challenge even the most experienced teacher. Given the challenging nature of these cases, it is important that you feel safe and comfortable expressing your opinions and ideas during discussions. The more supportive the environment created by instructors and peers, the more open you will be in sharing your ideas. It is likely during discussion that others will challenge your beliefs. This is a positive event because challenge provides the occasion to defend and consider your ideas in relation to the ideas of others. The challenge creates the opportunity to develop new and more complex schema. More complex schema will serve as a better foundation for the important decisions you will make as a teacher. The final chapter is a step-by-step guide for developing your own case study. Here you will describe, analyze, and solve a real student or classroom problem. The activities in the final chapter demonstrate your newly developed reflective problem-solving abilities.

All of the case studies found in this book are fictionalized accounts based on a kernel of reality that was used as an initial source for a story presenting an educational problem that new teachers are likely to encounter. I use case studies often in my classes, and many have been field-tested with my own students. Investigating controversial issues with my students, I am sometimes amazed by their responses and the way they think and reason about complex issues. My students are surprised when I explain that the cognitive levels of adults are as developmentally predictable and as documented as the growth and development of young children. They assume that growth in quality of thinking stops at age 12 with Piaget's formal operations. They also assume that development of thinking is either highly individualized, based on personality and experience or determined primarily by culture and social values. Not so! I have found the work of King and Kitchener (1994) and other researchers in cognitive development to be extremely helpful in understanding the levels of development that predict how my students think and solve problems. The case study rubrics are based on these developmental levels. The first and highest level of the rubric describes the problem-solving process as using many sources of evidence to find a solution, including theory, research, expert knowledge, student data, and direct personal experience. The second level of the rubric represents thinking that relies mainly on direct personal experience, and although it may include a bit of theory, research, and other abstract sources, their use is not systematic. The third level of the rubric represents positions based entirely on existing knowledge, preconceived ideas, stereotypes, and conventional wisdom that are not examined in relation to the evidence presented in the case study. You might ask how the responses from the three levels can be differentiated? This is difficult and only the respondent can accurately describe the sources for and the processes used in their evaluation. The rubrics are designed to provide feedback to you, the reader, to help you interpret the level of your own responses. While exploring the case studies, your skill in reflection and problem solving should improve. You may have believed that your teacher-preparation training was simply about lesson plans and content knowledge, but growth in understanding and thinking processes represented in this book is the most important (and exciting) aspect of your journey to become a teacher.

REFERENCE

King, P. M., & Kitchener, K. S. (1994). *Developing reflective judgment.* San Francisco: Jossey-Bass.

Case Study Number	*Case Study*	*Page Number*	*Grade Level*	*Case Focus*	*Primary Educational Topic*	*Secondary Topic*
1	Low achievement: Antonio Johnson	13	Middle school	Student	Low academic achievement	Diversity, medical problems, professional ethics
2	Learning disabilities: Charlie Yazzie	18	Upper elementary	Student	Learning disabilities	Diversity, diagnostic testing, expert/novice teachers
3	Low motivation: Hannah Wagner	24	Upper elementary	Student	Low motivation	School retention, Piaget's equilibrium/disequilibrium
4	Misbehaving students: Student teacher	29	Upper elementary/ middle school	Student teacher	Classroom management	Reflection, teacher stages of concern
5	Attention deficit/ hyperactive disorder: Gabe Silva	79	Early elementary	Student	Attention deficit/ hyperactive disorder	Classroom management, diversity structured observation, parent conferences
6	Underachievement: Lashandra Jones	86	High school	Student	Low academic achievement	Gifted education, diversity, parent conferences, extrinsic and intrinsic motivation, gender
7	Behavior disorder: William "Billy" Stark	90	Middle school	Student	Behavior disorder	Parent conferences, behavior management (rewards), Maslow's needs theory, constructivism
8	English as second language: Kitipitiyangkul Sisters	99	Early elementary	Student	Bilingual education	Diversity, teacher-parent interaction

Case Study Number	*Case Study*	*Page Number*	*Grade Level*	*Case Focus*	*Primary Educational Topic*	*Secondary Topic*
9	Reluctant reader: Amy Briggs	104	Early elementary	Student	Literacy education	Behavior management, parent conferences, teacher efficacy, low academic achievement
10	Inattentive children: Student teacher	117	Early elementary	Student teacher	Effective instruction	Student teaching conferencing
11	High-stakes assessment: Biology teacher	120	High school	Teacher	High-stakes assessment	Science education, school culture, administrative authority
12	Inappropriate scaffolding: Cassie Bright	126	Upper elementary/ middle school	Student	Instructional scaffolding	Writing instruction, gifted education, magic realism, gender
13	Mismatched assessment methods: Math teacher	132	High school	Teacher	Assessment methods	Math education, block scheduling, goals theory, cooperative learning, rubrics
14	Disruptive student: Morris Leonard	147	Middle school	Student	Classroom management	Intrinsic motivation theory, low academic achievement, gifted education
15	Black/White question: English teacher	152	High school	Teacher	Diversity	English education, racism, segregation, effective instructional techniques
16	Cultural conflict: Cindi Skillman	160	High school	Student	Cultural and socioeconomic issues	Low academic achievement, diversity, peer interactions, gender
17	Classroom holiday decorations: Elementary teacher	164	Early elementary	Teacher	Religion in the classroom	Administrative authority, diversity

PART I

INTRODUCTION AND CASE STUDY ANALYSIS

ONE

INTRODUCTION TO THE BOOK AND CASE STUDIES

BEFORE READING—REFLECTING ON JENNIFER'S STORY

Jennifer was small, delicate looking, and quiet. She had long brown hair and big brown eyes, and she giggled and was overcome with shyness when I spoke to her. She was somewhat immature compared to the other children, but she seemed to like school and adjusted well to the first-grade classroom. I clearly remember Jennifer from my first year as a teacher. Jennifer was learning to read and write in her first big educational adventure and didn't warrant my special notice until the school year was well underway. At that point, Jennifer's mother made an appointment with me to relate some happy news. It seemed that Jennifer had lost her father when she was a baby, and now her mother was preparing to remarry. The date was set, the wedding was planned, and Jennifer was to be a flower girl. Jennifer giggled and twisted excitedly on her mother's arm as the details of the wedding were described. Jennifer was also excited about her new daddy, who had already made plans to adopt her. All of this seemed the happiest of family circumstances, so I was surprised when Jennifer's work began to suffer. Jennifer stopped doing her assignments, and the work she did attempt was sloppy and incomplete. Curious, I began to watch her at her desk. Jennifer acted as if she were in a daze—rather than working on her math, reading, or writing a story, she daydreamed, doodled, and wiggled restlessly in her seat. More surprising than that, quiet Jennifer began to relate the most startling stories about her home life. When I asked Jennifer why she hadn't returned her reading assignment, she told me that her little brother was sick and might die so she couldn't do her work. Becoming suspicious, I decided to check out the story. At the end of the school day, I walked Jennifer to the corner where her new daddy picked her up. I asked Jennifer's dad about the sick little brother, and he turned in surprised to Jennifer—of course, Jennifer didn't have a brother, much less a sick one! Jennifer giggled and ducked her head. At some level, she seemed to know that she had played a great joke on me.

TEACHER STORIES

This incident had a happy ending, as soon Jennifer was back to her old self, participating in class and completing her work. I remember the incident because it taught me something very important about the fragility of learning. This was one of my first experiences in dealing with a student problem and being uncertain about how to handle it. Looking back, I now realize I was engaged in reflection in order to solve a classroom problem. At the time, I didn't know the word *reflection* or how reflection could be used to solve classroom problems. Years later, I understand the need for reflection—the process of "thinking like a teacher"—that as a new teacher I was struggling to teach myself. Intuitively, I knew that I shouldn't put additional pressure on Jennifer or punish her for her lack of effort. Somehow, I knew she was busy dealing with a difficult home situation, and I wanted to allow her time for that. All the while, as a first-year teacher, I was anxious about not assisting a child who had stopped learning, particularly when I didn't have any idea how long Jennifer's hiatus from learning would last. Happily, it was only for a few months, so I felt I made the right decision to give Jennifer space and to contact her parents about the unexpected change in her behavior.

I'm grateful to Jennifer because she taught me an important lesson about learning and how even in the happiest of circumstances a stressful event in a child's life can interrupt the learning process. It also caused me to wonder how children with horrendous home lives (several in that same classroom) ever learned anything at all. Jennifer, and all my students during those first few difficult years, taught me many important lessons about children, learning, and how to be sensitive to students with special needs. While these early experiences in the classroom taught me how to be an effective, practicing teacher they also provided me insight into how teachers reflect and how they solve classroom problems.

All teachers have stories like mine about Jennifer, and they enjoy telling these stories and relating their special meaning. From the earliest times, life stories have been important in understanding ourselves and relating the importance of what we do (MacIntyre, 1984). Some teacher educators believe that everyday classroom stories are important tools that teachers can use to learn about their teaching and the students they teach (Clandinin & Connelly, 1995; Knowles & Holt-Reynolds, 1991; Preskill & Jacobvitz, 2001). One way of using the impulse of storytelling is to formalize this natural process by analyzing and writing student case studies. Vivian Paley, a kindergarten teacher, wrote a series of books, including *White Teacher* (1979) and *The Boy Who Would be a Helicopter* (1990), that relates her story as a teacher and how she learned about being a teacher from her students.

This book uses teacher stories and the case study process as a tool to help beginning teachers explore the classroom, students, and learning in ways that are more natural and engaging than traditional educational textbooks. It uses classroom stories as the focus to explore common classroom issues such as discipline, student motivation, and the special needs of students. The next section describes this special type of teacher decision making and how individuals become thoughtful teachers.

REFLECTION AND HOW TO BECOME A THOUGHTFUL TEACHER

The purpose of this book is to provide beginning teachers practice with the skills needed to make good classroom decisions. Jackson (1986) tells us that classrooms are extremely complex and busy places. Teachers make dozens of daily classroom decisions. How does a teacher learn how to make these decisions? What can a teacher do to ensure that he or she is making decisions that will benefit students?

Case studies can be used as a tool to learn about the process of classroom problem solving. A case study typically describes a specific student or classroom problem—with the aim of solving the problem. This book provides both examples of case studies to analyze and a structure that the reader can use to develop his or her own classroom case studies. Practice in structured problem solving and reflection are important so that beginning teachers can develop into skilled professionals as recommended by national groups such as

Interstate New Teacher Assessment and Support Consortium (INTASC). Teacher standards developed by INTASC detail the knowledge, skills, attitudes, and beliefs teachers need to be effective in the classroom. These standards are extensive and require much thought and practice to allow beginning teachers to integrate them into daily classroom behaviors (Darling-Hammond, Wise, & Klein, 1995). Practice with the case study method can help new teachers begin to synthesize this knowledge into professional teaching behaviors. In addition, the PRAXIS Test and the *Principles of Learning and Teaching* (PLT) use classroom case histories as one determinate of a beginning teacher's pedagogical knowledge (ETS, 2001). Currently, states including Kentucky, South Carolina, and Kansas require the PLT as part of their certification requirements. New teachers need practice using this type of assessment format before they take an important test that will determine their qualifications for becoming a teacher.

Stake (2000) defined the case study method as the selection of a specific, unique, bounded system to be investigated. The case can be studied for a variety of reasons; in this book, cases serve as vehicles to investigate educational problems and issues. Stake describes how the narrative of the case provides an opportunity for vicarious experience, where readers expand their memories of happenings leading to increased awareness and understanding leading to the construction of new knowledge.

The use of case studies in teacher education is based on the research of educators such as Lee Shulman (1986). He advocated the use of case studies in education in the same manner that case studies are used to teach the practice of law. Law educators use case studies not to teach specific instances of the law but to argue for a broad application of how a law works. The particular case stands as a general example of how the law works, and it illustrates and serves as a model for new applications of that law. Shulman (1986) suggested that case studies could be used in the same way for teachers. He described how case studies representing typical classroom situations may serve as teaching tools to illustrate how teachers apply educational theory to make classroom decisions. He suggested that as prospective teachers practice the use of case studies and application of theory, they should develop a template or framework for how to think through tough classroom problems.

This framework will not provide the correct solution to every problem for new teachers—that is impossible—but it can help new teachers utilize experience more effectively by providing a way to better organize experiences in order to solve problems. Case studies provide new teachers with the processes of classroom problem solving that experienced teachers eventually learn through trial-and-error problem solving. Traditionally, new teachers have been left in isolation to figure out these problem-solving processes. The case study method gives new teachers the benefit of classroom experience and hopefully shortens the trial-and-error learning process. The case study is a way to provide a "leg up" in teacher development so prospective teachers become more effective more quickly in the classroom.

Most prospective teachers would readily agree that experience in an actual classroom is the best way to practice and demonstrate teaching skills. But while field experiences might be preferred by the prospective teacher, they also present a number of difficulties and limitations. For example, locations for sheltered field experiences may not be available to the extent that the prospective teacher might need. Also, it can be difficult to predict and control what happens in the field. For example, certain situations may never arise in the field to allow the new teacher to experience important instructional situations or specific student behavior. Or the instructional methods used in the field may not be the same as those advocated by the course instructor.

In addition, case studies offer a safety factor, where the decisions of an inexperienced prospective teacher will not harm an actual child. They offer opportunities for collaboration and deliberation with peers where prospective teachers are able to work together to share and solve a specific problem. Case studies allow the course instructor to tailor course experiences to specific classroom situations and course objectives. Overall, case studies allow deliberation, reflection, discussion, and collaboration that are not always possible in a real setting, where classroom decisions are often instantaneous and impossible to capture for examination. Case studies, although not as vivid and compelling as a real classroom, offer an alternative to field experiences that includes a degree of control, shared experience, and emotional safety impossible to duplicate in a real classroom setting. They offer a vicarious experience as an instructional alternative that can augment, although not replace, experience in real classrooms.

WHAT TO EXPECT

This book provides prospective teachers a variety of issues to discuss and skills to practice in order to begin their journey to become reflective problem solvers. Chapter 2 presents the reader with his or her first experience in using case studies to solve classroom and student problems. It provides a number of case studies to prompt the reader to explore the case study method. These first case studies are based on topics that research has shown are of universal concern for new and prospective teachers (Veenman, 1984). Chapters 3, 4, and 5 describe the professional foundations for skillful classroom problem solving. Chapter 3 addresses the topic of reflection, where reflection is described as a special way of thinking fundamental to the process of making good classroom decisions. Chapter 4 describes the process for developing an educational philosophy. This chapter explains that an educational philosophy provides the answers to *why* a teacher makes a particular instructional decision to select a textbook, to arrange the classroom in a certain fashion, or to administer a particular classroom management system. Educational philosophy includes the underlying values, beliefs, and dispositions that influence classroom decisions. Activities at the end of the chapter allow the reader to explore his or her own values, beliefs, and dispositions so that an educational philosophy can be developed as the basis for reflective classroom problem solving.

In Chapter 5, case studies of students with special needs are presented for analysis. According to Veenman (1984), providing instruction for students with differences—students with disabilities (physical, emotional, cognitive); difficulties in learning; or cultural, ethnic, and language differences—is a particular concern for new teachers. The cases present the common exceptionalities that a new teacher is likely to encounter—the conditions of attention deficit/hyperactivity disorder, underachievement, behavior disorder, and reluctant readers. The case studies of Chapter 6 portray the common but challenging educational issues of curriculum, instruction, and assessment. These case studies describe ordinary problems concerning what to teach, how to teach, and how to determine if students have learned. Although these are ordinary problems that all teachers face, they may be exceedingly difficult for new teachers to handle. Particularly, issues of evaluation in an era of "high stakes assessment" can be challenging for new teachers. Oftentimes, outside forces—such as state and national mandates, pressures to cover content, and overly prescriptive curriculum—can make teachers feel that they are not allowed to teach in the manner that is best for their students. This can be a source of frustration and unhappiness for excellent teachers, but there are ways to ameliorate this by negotiating outside demands with teacher philosophy and reflective problem solving. In Chapter 7, the context of the classroom is explored as an important consideration for making good classroom decisions. In the contextual view, the classroom is seen as a group of unique learners guided by a unique teacher who is ready to provide the best possible instruction to meet student needs. In Chapter 8, the reader will write his or her own case study using structured activities that allow case study development in a step-by-step manner. The reader is guided to explore a self-identified problem according to the problem-solving processes and knowledge gained from previous chapters.

Reflective questions and activities are provided in each chapter to help the reader personalize the information presented on each topic. They will also allow the reader to apply and integrate new knowledge in order to make it accessible for problem solving during case study development and analysis, and later in the classroom during field experiences and student teaching. The chapter exercises provide practice in the skills used to make reflective decisions and, hopefully, to help the prospective teacher avoid some of the pitfalls common to the novice stage of teacher development. Finally, Internet resources are listed at the end of each chapter to supplement the information explored in each chapter. Often a case study will only touch upon a complex topic that is of critical interest to teachers. Many topics deserve far more space than what is presented in this book. The Internet resources and printed references will provide sources where the reader can learn more about a topic of special import and interest.

END-OF-THE-CHAPTER REFLECTIVE ACTIVITY—WRITING A TEACHER STORY

The activity at the end of this chapter will start the reader on a journey of reflection in becoming a professional teacher and a reflective problem solver. Writing your own story of teaching will help you understand your beliefs and values about teaching and reveal your motivation for becoming a teacher. This is just the beginning for you, because, as teachers such as Vivian Paley (1990) and Parker Palmer (1998) describe, the journey to becoming a teacher can also be a journey to discover your truest self as a human being.

What is your teacher story? Do you have a story about an experience you can describe in which you were in a classroom situation or classroomlike situation? This might be a summer camp, Sunday school, an experience coaching sports, or even baby-sitting. Or, if you can't think of a teacher story, write a student story. Everyone remembers a special story about a time when they were a student. Write about an incident or occasion—happy or sad—that made an impression on you. Write a one- or two-page version of this story to share with others in the class. This introductory writing activity will prepare you for the writing you will do later in the book. If you are stuck, use the following prompts to guide the development of your story.

1. Describe what happened during the incident.
2. Why do you think you remember the incident?
3. Describe how you felt about it at the time. Did you share the incident with anyone?
4. Discuss how it affected you later in life. What did it teach you about school, teaching, or learning?

REFERENCES

Clandinin, J. D., & Connelly, M. F. (1995). *Teachers' professional knowledge landscapes.* New York: Teachers College Press.

Darling-Hammond, L., Wise, A. E., & Klein, S. P. (1995). *A license to teach: Building a profession for 21st century schools.* Boulder, CO: Westview Press.

Educational Testing Service. (2001). *PRAXIS test at a glance: Principles of learning and teaching.* Princeton, NJ: Author.

Jackson, P. (1986). *The practice of teaching.* New York: Teachers College Press.

Knowles, G. J., & Holt-Reynolds, D. (1991). Shaping pedagogies through personal histories in preservice teacher education. *Teachers College Record, 93*(1), 87–113.

MacIntyre, A. (1984). *After virtue.* Notre Dame, IN: University of Notre Dame Press.

Paley, V. (1979). *White teacher.* Cambridge, MA: Harvard University Press.

Paley, V. (1990). *The boy who would be a helicopter.* Cambridge, MA: Harvard University Press.

Palmer, P. J. (1998). *The courage to teach: Exploring the inner landscape of a teacher's life.* San Francisco: Jossey-Bass.

Preskill, S. L., & Jacobvitz, R. S. (2001). *Stories of teaching.* Upper Saddle River, NJ: Prentice Hall.

Shulman, L. S. (1986). Those who understand: Knowledge growth in teaching. *Educational Researcher, 15*(2), 4–14.

Stake, R. E. (2000). Case studies. In N. K. Denzin & Y. S. Lincoln (Eds.), *Handbook of qualitative research* (2nd ed., pp. 435–454). Thousand Oaks, CA: Sage Publications.

Veenman, S. (1984). Perceived problems of beginning teachers. *Review of Educational Research, 54*(2), 143–178.

INTERNET RESOURCES

Council of Chief State Officers

www.ccsso.org/projects/Interstate_New_Teacher_Assessment_and_Support_Consortium/

Council of Chief State Officers developed the INTASC teacher standards. The home page describes what the Council is and what it does for the national educational community. It is described as a nationwide nonprofit organization that sets policy and supports research for elementary and secondary education.

INTASC Teacher Standards

www.ccsso.org/content/pdfs/corestrd.pdf

A Web site of the Interstate New Teacher Assessment and Support Consortium (INTASC) Teacher Standards. This set of teacher standards is used in many states to determine the quality of a teacher's classroom performance. The INTASC teacher standards were developed by the Council of Chief State Officers.

PRAXIS Tests (ETS)

www.ets.org/praxis/prxtest.html#prxiiplt

This Web site provides a listing of the PRAXIS tests, including the PLT (Principles of Learning and Teaching) and the subject matter tests. Information is provided about the topics found on each test from the *Test at a Glance* manuals (which are free and downloadable in PDF format).

www.ets.org/praxis/prxstate.html

This page provides a list of PRAXIS test requirements according to state certification requirements. Most states now require some type of testing before teachers are certified for the classroom. Most states use the ETS exams to meet their testing requirements.

Teacher Stories

www.lessonplanspage.com/index.html
www.useyourheadteach.gov.uk/teachers_stories/index.html
www.teacheruniverse.com/community/teacherstories/moments.html

These Web sites provide stories about teachers that will inspire or inform you about the profession of teaching and what teaching means to individuals.

TWO

LEARNING TO USE CASE STUDIES TO SOLVE CLASSROOM PROBLEMS

In Chapter 2, four case studies will be presented and analyzed to teach specific lessons about how to use case studies to solve classroom problems. By design it is anticipated that you will be confronted by new ideas about classrooms and teaching. You should be patient with yourself as you learn to examine the world from the eyes of a teacher rather than from your current viewpoint—the eyes of a student.

CASE STUDY ONE—LOW ACHIEVEMENT: ANTONIO JOHNSON (PART I)

It is the third week of school and Antonio's teacher is already concerned about his academic progress. Antonio is an undersized African American male in the seventh grade with significant academic and skill deficits. Antonio is thin and looks half-starved, with the tired eyes of someone lacking sleep. Antonio's clothes are big for him, and while clean, they are wrinkled and do not match. Antonio frequently comes to school tardy and is also often absent. One of the other teachers mentioned to the seventh-grade homeroom teacher that Antonio's mother worked a lot and his dad didn't seem to live with the family anymore. In homeroom, Antonio doesn't seem to be aware of how far behind the rest of the seventh-grade class he is.

When his teacher tries to encourage or admonish him, he gets angry and pouts and withdraws from the rest of the class. During these sessions, he slumps in his chair, hiding his face in his jacket, or he puts his head on the desk and closes his eyes, refusing to discuss the situation. Also, while Antonio doesn't seem interested in completing his work in class, he does like to talk and joke with the other students, distracting them from their assignments. He becomes particularly animated with a group of pretty, popular girls, who, at best, seem only to tolerate his company, with his silly jokes, loud displays, and horsing around to gain the girls' attention. When his teacher sends work home to be completed, the results are not any better than Antonio's efforts at school. When asked, Antonio claims he didn't have time to do his work or he lost it. When the homeroom teacher checked with his other teachers, they reported poor academic performance and noted his immature and socially clumsy behavior with other students. The last straw was an incident the homeroom teacher heard about in the teacher's lounge. Another teacher claimed that during a basketball warm-up exercise, Antonio was accidentally hit on the leg with a ball. Afterward, even though the physical education teacher and school nurse checked his leg, which wasn't even bruised, Antonio screamed, cried, and carried on about the pain. He insisted on calling his mother at work, who picked him up and took him home.

Hearing about this incident, Antonio's teacher decides she is at the end of her patience with him. At this time, she feels she needs advice or additional resources to deal with Antonio's behavior and lack of achievement. Based on this preliminary information, what would you determine to be Antonio's problem? How would you attempt to help him? What other information would you like about his situation?

Your responses:

___

___

___

___

CASE STUDY ONE—LOW ACHIEVEMENT: ANTONIO JOHNSON (PART II)

Review your response according to the rubric below:

Evidencing high-quality classroom insight and teacher knowledge—if you suggested that Antonio might have a medical condition that has delayed his academic and social development. To provide this response, you must have had a similar experience or have great insight into student behavior and motivation. Antonio's condition could be one that leaves him unsure of himself with his peers, behind in his academics, and overly sensitive to pain.
Evidencing emerging classroom insight and teacher knowledge—if you suggested the need to delay any advice or action until you discover more details about Antonio's situation, including talking with the school counselor, nurse, principal, and parents.
Evidencing the need for additional classroom insight and teacher knowledge—if you attributed Antonio's behavior to his being on drugs or his parents neglecting him or by determining that Antonio is poor and comes from a bad neighborhood, has a learning or behavior disorder, or has a low IQ. Those are judgments based on cultural stereotypes, and you do not have enough information from the case study to draw such significant conclusions. Students with special needs and problems benefit from teachers who are willing to investigate their situation and who don't jump to judgmental conclusions based on rumors and limited information.

A response that matches the lowest level of the rubric suggests that you need more practice in reflecting upon classroom situations and using teacher knowledge to make informed and professional decisions for students. This is not a surprising finding. The purpose of this book and of case study analysis in particular is to provide exactly those skills. The reason for including this chapter on learning to use case studies at the beginning of the book is to persuade you to develop your skills in reflective problem solving in order to make professional classroom and student decisions. If your response matches the middle level of the rubric, you have some insight into the situation, but additional knowledge and experience would be extremely helpful to fully develop your evaluation skills in order to make the best determination for the student. If your answer matches the top level of the rubric, you have the necessary insight for solving classroom problems along with the background knowledge required by teachers to make mature, informed, and professional decisions. This level is extremely rare to find in a beginning teacher, so don't be discouraged if your answer better matches the other two rubric levels.

FOLLOW-UP TO CASE STUDY ONE

Antonio's teacher, after a careful investigation in which she spoke with the school counselor, nurse, principal, and Antonio's parents, discovered that Antonio was currently in remission from leukemia and had just returned to school. During Antonio's 2-year illness, he had been in and out of the hospital, where he received many treatments, including a bone marrow transplant. Although he had been provided homebound tutoring, he was often too ill or depressed to make much academic progress. Antonio's medical treatments, while successful, had left his family with a large medical debt requiring his father to work out of town for additional income and his mother to work full-time. Antonio's mother reported that Antonio was overjoyed to be in school again, leading a regular life and interacting with his peers. She recognized that Antonio was behind in academics, but she didn't have the heart to push or nag him about his studies when she was happy to just have him alive and excited about life again.

At this point you may feel that you have been tricked or set up with this case study. Don't be overly alarmed if your reaction to Antonio's story reflects the low category. The reality is that even experienced teachers often jump to conclusions about students without checking their facts. The case study of Antonio was used to demonstrate that becoming a responsible, professional teacher means being sensitive to students and their situations. It also means that teachers do not judge students according to preconceived notions, stereotypical beliefs, or generalizations—particularly racist or sexist attitudes. These elements are all a part of our culture, and they can influence our thinking and behavior without our awareness. To some extent, it is the nature of human beings to love gossip, to talk with others in a dramatic fashion, and to pass on juicy information. But for a teacher to do so (though many veteran teachers are guilty of this) is unprofessional, unethical, and potentially harmful to students and their families.

To reassure you that other prospective teachers make preconceived, unwarranted responses, following are responses to this case study from the students in my own classes.

Response One
First of all I'd like to meet Antonio's parents to see what is happening in his home life. I am afraid that Antonio is either neglected and/or verbally abused at home.

Antonio severely withdraws when "called down" in class, suggesting that he is maybe used to being verbally abused when "called down" at home.
Response Two
I think Antonio is attention deficit. He feels the need to be loud, compulsive, and distractive because getting in trouble provides him with a way to gain the attention he needs.
Response Three
Antonio is possibly ADHD, LD, or BD. He might possibly be a victim of child abuse from his father. Antonio might not be receiving proper parenting at home (mother gone, no father). This means the TV has become his baby-sitter, and he hasn't developed an attention span for school.
Response Four
Antonio may be living in a single-parent environment in which education is not emphasized. He may live in a bad neighborhood where survival is most important.
Response Five
I would speculate that Antonio's home life is the cause of the behavior at school. It could be that Antonio is tired because he cares for himself and other siblings while his mother is at work.
Response Six
Because of his wild reaction to getting hurt, I would speculate that maybe his mother's boyfriend was being physically abusive to Antonio. Because he comes into class with tired eyes is also alarming because it lets me know he doesn't sleep very well at night, maybe afraid of a lurking danger in the household.

Notice how the students make judgments about Antonio based on limited and unreliable information—teacher gossip really. Notice how the students jump to conclusions about Antonio's home life, giving him siblings, an abusive boyfriend for his mother, and a dangerous neighborhood to live in. Notice how they attribute Antonio's behavior to learning and behavior disorders without consultation with specialists or a diagnosing process. None of these conclusions could be drawn from the information provided in the case study. Is it possible that stereotyping is the source of these judgments and that if Antonio had been described as a white child rather than African American these same conclusions would not have been drawn?

All students deserve a teacher with an open heart and an open mind. No child needs a judgmental teacher ready to believe the worst about the student and his or her family. To avoid judgments, teachers need to take an understanding perspective rather than a judging one. A *judging perspective* tends to limit the problem-solving process because it is immediately assumed that because a solution has already been found, no other means of investigation are needed and no other solutions need to be considered. On the other hand, if the teacher has a *perspective of understanding,* he or she is flexible and ready to consider the problem in a variety of ways and to explore a number of solutions to help the student.

Lesson One in Using Case Studies

Never make judgments about students without checking the facts with reliable sources. Never label, belittle, or otherwise speak unkindly about students and their parents.

FINAL ACTIVITY FOR CASE STUDY ONE

Work in small groups to discuss ways that Antonio's teacher can help him catch up academically with his classmates. Also, how can Antonio work on his social skills so that he relates more appropriately with his peers? Could Antonio's parents be enlisted to help develop solutions to help him?

Your responses:

____

____

____

____

While reading this second case study, take the knowledge you have just learned from the Antonio case study and apply it to Charlie's situation. Don't be afraid to respond; just make sure you are not making unfounded judgments about Charlie.

CASE STUDY TWO—LEARNING DISABILITIES: CHARLIE YAZZIE (PART I)

When Richard Garcia learned that he would have a new student in his fifth-grade classroom, he was excited about the prospect. The principal told him that Charlie Yazzie had lived his entire life on a reservation and was fluent in both Navajo and English. Charlie's father had just moved to the city for a job in a new window manufacturing plant. Richard looked forward to learning about Navajo culture and being able to share that knowledge with his students who were of either Anglo or Hispanic descent.

Richard saw that Charlie was shy his first day of class. Charlie was dressed in jeans and a plaid shirt, and he stared at Richard with big brown eyes. His thick, dark hair looked impossible to comb. Charlie was small for his age, and Richard was immediately worried about his ability to play sports. He wondered if Charlie played baseball or basketball, because sports were very important to the other fifth-grade boys, and playing sports would help Charlie to fit into the group and make friends with the other boys. Richard was immediately sympathetic to Charlie and the problems of adjusting to life in the city and making friends at a new school. As a first step, Richard assigned one of the more popular and friendlier boys, Sean, to show Charlie around the school, to eat lunch together, and to play with during recess. To Richard's surprise, Charlie ditched Sean on the playground and hung around with the girls. The girls were jumping rope and Charlie tried to join in. This was to the hilarity of the girls as he constantly missed jumps, got tangled in the rope, and finally fell down.

Charlie's unexpected social choice was just the start of a catalog of surprises for Richard. Richard didn't know what to expect in terms of Charlie's academic skills. He was unfamiliar with the Navajo reservation system and had no idea of the type of curriculum or standards that were provided. According to Charlie's records, his grades were average and below, with some indication of problems in reading. To find out about Charlie's skills, Richard required the entire class to write a personal narrative about a recent important event that had changed their lives. The students groaned at the assignment, but Richard was used to that, and he encouraged the students with prewriting activities where they brainstormed ideas and worked in pairs to select topics and begin writing. Charlie didn't seem interested in this assignment or the topic. With his recent move to the city, Richard thought the topic was perfect for Charlie to explore. Richard tried to help Charlie by asking him questions about his old school and home, probing him to see how they compared to his new experiences. Charlie just mumbled and shrugged his shoulders. Giving up on that topic, Richard told Charlie he could write about anything of interest to him. Charlie finally decided to write about the last time his dad had taken him to a Navajo ceremonial. After spending several class periods writing, the draft that Charlie finally turned in dismayed Richard. The smudged, torn paper was full of bizarre spellings, letter reversals, sentence fragments, and an incomprehensible story line. Charlie's paper looked like the work of a remedial first or second grader. When Richard conferenced with Charlie about the paper, he found that Charlie could barely read it. He mispronounced and made up words and changed the story every time he read it. A frustrated Charlie told Richard that he didn't understand what he wanted him to do and that he hated to read and write. Undaunted and in an attempt to relate to Charlie's experiences, Richard searched until he found several books of Navajo legends and folklore. Charlie shrugged at them and said he already knew those stories, leaving them untouched at his desk.

After 6 weeks, Richard mentally tallied his assessment of Charlie. Charlie couldn't spell, write, or read anything but the most basic primers. His math skills were pretty good, he made Cs and some Bs on his papers, but he was sloppy and missed answers due to simple errors and not following directions. Observing him on the playground, Charlie didn't seem the least bit interested in joining the other boys when they played baseball but preferred instead to play with the girls who, at best, tolerated him. They sent him on errands, made him dress up, and ordered him around. As Richard had feared, because Charlie didn't play sports, the other boys teased him, called him names, and ostracized him from their games and company.

When Richard asked the physical education teacher about Charlie, he said he was willing to take part in all the activities, but he had failed every written test given so far. The art teacher described him as eager but messy and unable to follow directions and complete a project. The music teacher said he loved to sing, but he had trouble with the written music tests.

What do you think Richard Garcia should do about Charlie?

Your responses:

____

____

____

____

CASE STUDY TWO—LEARNING DISABILITIES: CHARLIE YAZZIE (PART II)

Review your response according to the following rubric:

Evidencing high-quality classroom insight and teacher knowledge—if you suggested that Richard Garcia should contact Charlie's parents and his principal in order to begin the process of making a special education referral. Richard has enough evidence of Charlie's academic problems to recognize that he and Charlie both need help. You recognized that Charlie wasn't likely to make progress without a specific diagnosis of the problem and outside help.
Evidencing emerging classroom insight and teacher knowledge—if you suggested that Charlie's academic difficulties were due to his Navajo heritage or language problems. The narrative says that Charlie is fluent in both languages, but the fact that Charlie is from the Navajo culture has distracted you from the source of Charlie's real problem. This judgment may reflect a subtle form of prejudice where a student's "difference" blinds the teacher to a real problem that is unrelated to cultural or other types of differences.
Evidencing the need for additional classroom insight and teacher knowledge—if you determined that Richard should not take any action with Charlie and that he should allow the situation to continue on its present course. The classroom evidence is contrary to this, as his learning deficits seem to be significant and of long standing. Richard has carefully observed Charlie, and he has collected enough preliminary data and is concerned enough about Charlie's learning difficulties to believe that the situation is not going to get better without outside intervention.

FOLLOW-UP TO CASE STUDY TWO

Based on the information that Richard had already collected about Charlie and from several weeks of instructional interventions, Richard made a special education referral to have Charlie tested for a learning disability. After obtaining permission from his parents, the special education team reviewed Charlie's entire school history, interviewed his parents and teachers, and observed Charlie in several of his classes. The team administered the Woodcock-Johnson III achievement test and the WISC IV individual intelligence test along with reviewing samples of Charlie's work from class. It was determined that, because Charlie's IQ was somewhat above normal but his performance on achievement tests was much lower than would be expected compared to his IQ and his peers, it was highly likely that Charlie was learning disabled with difficulty in decoding and processing language.

Hopefully, for this case study you did not make any rash judgments about Charlie, but it is also hoped that you were not so "psychologically traumatized" by the experience of the last case study that you failed to intervene for a student who was obviously struggling with normal classwork. Don't be too hard on yourself if you didn't suggest an intervention. Researchers (Carter, Cushing, Sabers, Stein, & Berliner, 1988) have found that there are measurable differences between what novice teachers and expert teachers notice in a classroom situation. If you failed to recognize that Charlie needed to be referred for help, this may be due to a lack of experience. One of the goals of this book is to help you gain vicarious experience using case studies so that when you are in a real classroom situation, it will be more likely that you will react as an experienced teacher. In determining what to do about Charlie, if you review the processes that Richard Garcia undertook to help Charlie, you will see that he first observed Charlie for several weeks to allow him to adapt to a new classroom. Once he saw that Charlie was experiencing problems with routine classroom assignments, he adapted assignments to address Charlie's needs and to determine the source of his problems (the writing assignment). Richard attempted to find materials from Charlie's culture that he might find interesting (the Navajo books). He worked with Charlie on an individual basis to gain more insight about him (individual writing conference). Richard then checked with other teachers (not to gossip about a student) to see how he functioned in other school situations. After collecting all of this evidence, Richard then made the special education referral to see what teachers with more experience working with learning difficulties thought about Charlie. The team reviewed Charlie's complete school history to make sure this was not just a temporary problem or an issue of adjustment to a new school. They interviewed his parents and other teachers who worked with Charlie, and finally, they administered tests to obtain objective data about Charlie's learning capabilities. This long process is described here to convince you how much time and effort is needed to diagnose students with problems like Charlie's.

The problem-solving process presented in this book relies on the collection of academic data, student observation, and the use of a variety of evidence to make determinations about student learning and behavior difficulties. An important part of becoming a teacher who is a reflective problem solver is to learn what is needed to make responsible decisions about students.

Lesson Two in Using Case Studies

Use data about student achievement and behavior when determining a strategy to help students who have problems. This same process should also be used to improve overall classroom management, organization, and instruction.

FINAL ACTIVITY FOR CASE STUDY TWO

Using your prior knowledge from courses that describe the characteristics of learning disabled (LD) students and the use of instructional interventions that will help them to compensate for their disabilities, work in small groups to determine how you can provide accommodations for Charlie so that he can be successful in the regular classroom. Do you think Charlie's parents would be willing to help?

Your responses:

____

____

For your third case study, consider the following student and how her teacher should work with her to solve her classroom difficulties.

CASE STUDY THREE—LOW MOTIVATION: HANNAH WAGNER (PART I)

Hannah has been sitting at her desk for nearly half an hour doing nothing, as far as her teacher Helene Weinstock can tell. Mrs. Weinstock urges Hannah to try one of the long division problems she is supposed to be working on. "I can't," claims Hannah without even looking at the problem the teacher is pointing to. She adds, "I don't understand it." The frustrated Mrs. Weinstock replies, "But I just went over a problem like it on the board—weren't you listening?" "I don't understand," Hannah repeats. The teacher goes through a long-division problem step-by-step, asking questions along the way. Hannah answers most of the questions correctly. She obviously has at least some understanding of the problem, Mrs. Weinstock thinks. "See, you know how to do these kinds of problems," she observes to Hannah. "Why don't you try one on your own now?" "I don't know how!" Hannah stubbornly declares. "But you knew the right answers to all my questions," the teacher responds. "I just guessed" is Hannah's ready reply. Not to be fooled, the teacher concludes, "I think you know how to do these, and I want you to try at least four of the problems. I'll come back and check on you later."

Mrs. Weinstock has the last word and turns her attention to another student, leaving Hannah alone with her division problems. Later, she passes by Hannah's desk and observes no progress. Hannah is staring into space and tapping her gnawed pencil. The scene just described is repeated many times, and the end result is an exasperated teacher and a student who interprets the teacher's despair as confirmation of her own lack of ability to learn.

Hannah is in the fourth grade, and with her current level of poor achievement, it is likely she will repeat the fourth grade. Hannah has long, stringy, dirty-looking blond hair. Her skin is extremely fair and her eyes have purplish circles under them. Her clothes and general appearance are unkempt. Because her academic performance is uniformly poor, Hannah is regarded by her classmates as one of the classroom "dummies." The other fourth-grade girls show distain and impatience with Hannah's efforts to fit in. They have known Hannah since kindergarten, and she has always been like this. So quiet, so wimpy, so unattractive, never having anything clever or fun to contribute. They tolerate her because the teachers insist, but secretly they call her "noodle" for her lack of initiative and her stringy hair. The boys in the fourth grade just ignore her.

Hannah is not disruptive. She is not socially integrated into the classroom and therefore is not tempted to spend her time talking and socializing. She is not aggressive, and rather than acting out, calling attention to herself, or interfering with her classmates, she sits quietly all day, every day, spending much of her time gazing into space and making doodles on small pieces of paper that she hides if the teacher walks by. She makes few demands on the teacher, and if she doesn't understand the assignment, she sits quietly staring at her paper. Hannah perceives no reason to ask questions because she does not expect to understand. She doesn't raise her hand because she has nothing of value to contribute, and who would listen to her anyway?

Hannah seems to have developed a self-perception of being incompetent in every fourth-grade skill and ability. She has convinced herself that she is unable to master any new academic material. Failure is inevitable, so "Why try?" she reasons.

When Mrs. Weinstock checked Hannah's academic records at the beginning of the year, she was dismayed. Since kindergarten, Hannah's grades ranged from poor to mediocre, and her current achievement was two grade levels below in most academic subjects. In the third grade, Hannah was tested for learning disabilities and none were found; her IQ was normal. Given this evidence and in spite of her lack of progress, Mrs. Weinstock knows that Hannah is capable of much more than she seems. When Mrs. Weinstock talks with Hannah about her assignments and works directly with her, Hannah evidences understanding of the material. Hannah just lacks initiative and seems incapable of working independently, as she gives up when she is faced with the smallest obstacles. Because she is so unattractive and frustrating to deal with, Mrs. Weinstock suspects that Hannah has been overlooked or ignored by her other teachers.

Hannah has been in Mrs. Weinstock's classroom for almost an entire year, and yet as the school year comes to a close, Mrs. Weinstock is frustrated with Hannah and with herself for not trying harder with her and for not being any closer to understanding her lack of learning and effort.

Mrs. Weinstock knows that the principal will ask for a recommendation to retain Hannah in the fourth grade for another year, and she is not sure how she will respond.

What do you think Mrs. Weinstock should do about Hannah?

Your responses:

____

____

____

____

CASE STUDY THREE—LOW MOTIVATION: HANNAH WAGNER (PART II)

Review your response according to the following rubric:

> **Evidencing high-quality classroom insight and teacher knowledge—**if you suggested that Hannah has a motivation problem that keeps her from performing academically. You could have written this book if you were able to cite a motivation theory such as "learned helplessness" and make suggestions about ways that Mrs. Weinstock could help Hannah based on that theory.

Evidencing emerging classroom insight and teacher knowledge—if you are confused about what to do about Hannah, but you suggested that Mrs. Weinstock should continue to work with Hannah to discover why she isn't learning, why she doesn't try to learn, and why she feels she doesn't have anything to contribute. A truly compassionate teacher doesn't give up on students but continues to try until the student passes out of her hands and into the hands of another teacher.

Evidencing the need for additional classroom insight and teacher knowledge—if you suggested that Mrs. Weinstock should continue as she has for the rest of the school year and then recommend that Hannah be retained in fourth grade for another year. Retention will have a devastating effect on Hannah, who already believes she is incapable of learning. This will verify her lack of ability and confirm that she deserves the label of "dummy."

FOLLOW-UP TO CASE STUDY THREE

Mrs. Weinstock thought about Hannah and her situation over the weekend and decided that for the rest of the school year she would give Hannah special attention and try to discover the reasons for Hannah's lack of effort. Mrs. Weinstock would review everything she had learned about motivation theory in her graduate courses and consider what to do for Hannah for the rest of the year. She would *not* recommend retention for Hannah to the principal, and she would share everything she learned about Hannah with the teacher next year.

To help the reader better understand Hannah's situation, Chapter 4 will address theories of learning and motivation and how they explain student behavior and help teachers make informed decisions about how to help students. It may seem unfair to you that the case study of Hannah required knowledge that has not yet been presented to you. One of the reasons for providing case studies early in the book is to demonstrate gaps in the reader's knowledge. If you feel that you have been unfairly set up by the case studies, or more accurately that you simply don't have the knowledge you need to make the appropriate responses, don't be discouraged; the case studies were designed for that exact purpose. The theories of researchers such as Piaget (1972) have found that true learning only occurs when the students experience a need to develop new understanding. The term Piaget used for this state was "disequilibrium." Disequilibrium means that the learner is uncomfortable with current understanding and, as a result, is compelled to change that understanding to make sense of a new situation. In this case, if you feel dissatisfied with your current responses to the case study problems, this state of disequilibrium will compel you to learn more so that you can make better responses. Often, disequilibrium is associated with negative or uneasy feelings. If you have such feelings, know that they are natural; when you are able to reach equilibrium again by adjusting your understanding, a feeling of exhilaration may follow. This exhilaration is often described as a lightbulb coming on when something new and important is learned or realized.

Think of these case studies as pretests to help you ascertain what you know and don't know about classrooms and students. If you "failed" the pretest, this simply demonstrates that you need the instruction that will follow. Rather than being discouraged, you can look forward to new ways of looking at classrooms and solving problems.

Lesson Three in Using Case Studies

Use learning and motivation theory to understand student behavior and to help you decide what you should do to assist a student who is not learning.

FINAL ACTIVITY FOR CASE STUDY THREE

Work in small groups to discuss ways in which Hannah's teacher can help her feel more confident about her learning and interactions with peers. These may include ideas such as asking Hannah and the other students to keep a journal about their learning, which may provide insight into Hannah's views about her abilities. Such a classroom investigation could also provide clues about motivational triggers that would encourage Hannah to start trying again. Many students experience motivation problems—maybe you have insight from when you were an elementary student.

Your responses:

____

____

There is one final case study to examine before moving to the content portion of the book. This fourth case study demonstrates that a case doesn't have to be about one particular student and a single problem. A case study can be used to illustrate a teacher, classroom, or instructional problem. This case study is about Amy, a student teacher. As you read, try to determine where Amy went wrong during her student teaching experience and what her next steps should be.

CASE STUDY FOUR—MISBEHAVING STUDENTS: STUDENT TEACHER (PART I)

By the end of her student teaching experience Amy often thought of the old adage of "not smiling until Christmas." Amy, who had a friendly, likable personality and sunny outlook on life, couldn't believe that by the end of the semester she hated the thought of being in a classroom any longer than she had to be. Amy had begun her student teaching with high expectations and enthusiasm for becoming a teacher. Then she met her sixth-grade class. At first the situation didn't seem too bad. The students were friendly and interested in learning about her, and they all wanted her attention. They asked many questions about her personal life—they wanted to know if she was married, if she had children, or if she had a boyfriend. They asked for her help during assignments, rushed to sit with her at lunch, and competed to stand next to her and chat during recess. Amy loved the attention the students showed her, and she loved that she had won over the students so easily. At this point in her student teaching placement, Amy had been observing her cooperating teacher helping small groups of students work on activities and answering individual student questions. She couldn't wait until she took over the classroom.

Looking back, Amy realized she should have anticipated trouble. Mr. Shannon, her cooperating teacher, claimed that this particular group of sixth graders, while bright and capable, were the rowdiest group that he had taught in his long career. Amy assumed the problem was Mr. Shannon, an old grump who didn't understand how students think and what they are like these days. He spoke in a monotone that put Amy to sleep, and all he cared about was covering the material and meeting his lesson objectives every day. He posted the objectives on the board in the morning, and at the end of the day he talked to the students about what they had accomplished, and if the class had misbehaved and missed a lesson, he discussed how they would make up the work the following day. Amy observed that Mr. Shannon often had to stop during a lesson to quiet students, and he sometimes sent students to the back of the room for discipline so that he could keep teaching.

Amy knew she had a friendly manner, a better delivery, and more exciting lesson ideas than Mr. Shannon. Amy assumed that, because the students liked her, this affection would translate into cooperation during her teaching. Amy was lucky the students loved her; she had earned their trust, and she reasoned that they would want to please her and help her when she began teaching the entire class. For her first lesson, when her university coordinator would observe her teaching, Amy worked hard to gather materials and plan an exciting activity. On the day of the lesson, it was the shock of her life when the students acted completely out of control. Her science lesson was complicated and used a lot of materials, including water and foam balls. She felt that the students took advantage of her just because she explained the assignment wrong, and when the activity didn't work as expected, they started splashing water on each other and throwing the balls around the room. Half an hour into the lesson, when things had completely fallen apart, Amy's university supervisor stopped the lesson. She and Amy left the classroom and went to a conference room to talk.

What do you think Amy will tell the university supervisor?

Your responses:

____

____

____

____

CASE STUDY FOUR—MISBEHAVING STUDENTS: STUDENT TEACHER (PART II)

Review your responses according to the following rubric:

Evidencing high-quality classroom insight and teacher knowledge—if you recognized that Amy tried to be a friend to her students rather than their teacher. You understand that the proper role for a teacher is to be concerned and responsible for student learning, not acquire new friends.
Evidencing emerging classroom insight and teacher knowledge—if you suggested that Amy needs to develop control of the classroom through her authority as a teacher rather than to depend on student affection to maintain classroom discipline. You understand that students will at times misbehave, and it is the teacher's responsibility to maintain order.
Evidencing the need for additional classroom insight and teacher knowledge—if you think it is the student's fault for misbehaving. If you feel that her students have betrayed Amy, you may be at the stage of teacher development where your chief concerns are of being liked by students and how you are evaluated by supervisors.

FOLLOW-UP TO CASE STUDY FOUR

When Amy and her university supervisor were alone, Amy launched into a tirade against the students. She explained how hard she had worked to plan the lesson and how much time and expense it took to gather the materials. She had planned this particular lesson because it was a topic she was familiar with and she knew it would be a lot of fun. She couldn't understand how they could treat her this way after all her hard work. She couldn't understand why they had acted like such brats and humiliated her during her observation. Amy asked her supervisor what would happen to her grade because she had to stop the lesson. Amy wanted to know if she could still get an A in her student teaching.

The university supervisor cautioned Amy to think about her responsibility in the situation. She agreed the students misbehaved, but the directions for the activity were unclear, and she wanted to know if Amy had a back-up plan in case the lesson did not go as expected. Amy sadly shook her head. The supervisor asked Amy to think about what she should do differently the next time she taught the lesson. A tearful Amy said, "Maybe this means I shouldn't be a teacher after all." Her supervisor said, "Maybe so, but I don't think you have given yourself or the students a fair chance to determine that." Once again, the supervisor asked Amy to think about a plan for how she would teach the lesson next time. Amy said she was afraid to try the lesson because she couldn't trust the students to use the materials or work together. Persisting, the supervisor asked Amy her plans for how she would take charge of the classroom and establish her authority as a teacher with the students. An emotionally bruised Amy shook her head; she didn't know.

If the reader is feeling critical about Amy and her behavior, consider that teacher development theory explains and describes Amy's reaction and why she reacted as she did to the students' behavior. Fuller (1969) describes three stages of concern that are characteristic of teachers. Amy is in the first stage, where her primary concerns are being liked by students, being evaluated by supervisors, and maintaining classroom control. Amy's problem at this point is not that she made a mistake with her lesson—every teacher does that—but that she refuses to reflect on the events of the lesson. Amy's supervisor knows that Amy will need help to move to the next stage of development if she is going to be an effective, confident teacher. In order to do that, Amy will have to reflect on the events of her student teaching and plan a more mature way to interact with the students. Research has shown that teachers who do not reflect do not grow. Amy's unhappy situation leads us to the final lesson about the analysis and use of case studies to solve classroom and student problems.

Lesson Four in Using Case Studies

Use reflection to help you decide how to make changes to your classroom and to help students. Learn how to be reflective, because teachers grow and develop their teaching by reflecting on their classroom experiences.

It is the premise of this book that teachers grow and improve through being reflective. Chapter 3 will describe this reflective process and how you can consider your own situation along with further examination of Amy's situation.

Following is a review of the lessons learned and what we have discovered about case studies in this chapter.

- **Lesson One**: Never make rash judgments about students without checking the facts with reliable sources. Never label, belittle, or otherwise speak unkindly about students and their parents.
- **Lesson Two**: Use data about student achievement and behavior to make the best determination of how to help students who have problems.
- **Lesson Three**: Use educational theory to understand and make decisions about how to assist students and solve classroom problems.
- **Lesson Four**: Learn how to be reflective when solving problems and how to recognize the importance of reflection in solving classroom problems and for long-term teacher development.

These four lessons should be taken into consideration when case studies are analyzed and solutions to case study problems are considered.

REFERENCES

Carter, K., Cushing, K., Sabers, D., Stein, P., & Berliner, D. (1988). Expert-novice differences in perceiving and processing visual classroom information. *Journal of Teacher Education, 39*(3), 25–31.

Fuller, F. (1969). Concerns of teachers: A developmental conceptualization. *American Educational Research Journal, 6*(2), 207–226.

Piaget, J. (1972). *The psychology of intelligence.* Totowa, NJ: Littlefield & Adams.

INTERNET RESOURCES

Classroom Management

www.ez2bsaved.com/class_manage.htm

This site claims to provide the biggest and best collection of classroom management resources—a list of 694 sites.

http://inset.ul.ie/cm/

This Irish Web site is a systematic and thorough investigation of classroom management issues for new teachers. It includes the following major topics: preparedness, preventative management, supportive management, and pupil misbehavior. It provides interactive activities in which teachers may record opinions and read the opinions of others.

Expert Versus Novice Teachers

http://216.239.37.104/search?q=cache:DAPEN0tlygQJ:atea.cqu.edu.au/content/know_base/downloads/allendlkb.rtf+expert+teachers+novice+teachers&hl=en&ie=UTF-8

This online paper describes the importance of reflection and how the investigator found that the recall of classroom events is different for expert and novice teachers. This is a real research study that is somewhat hard to read but provides interesting background information about the topic.

http://carbon.cudenver.edu/public/education/edschool/cog/bibs/cindy2.html

A summary of a David Berliner paper that examines the routines of expert teachers versus novice teachers in order to observe and understand differences in their behavior. Berliner has researched expert teachers extensively and would be a good source for other articles on this topic.

Learning Disabilities

www.ldonline.org/

This *LD Online* site is for parents and teachers. It offers basic and in-depth information about learning disabilities as well as strategies for teachers and news about changes in laws and mandates for LD students.

www.ldanatl.org/

This Web site of The Learning Disabilities Association of America (LDA) offers resources and membership in this advocacy group. LDA is a nonprofit grassroots organization whose members are individuals with learning disabilities, their families, and the professionals who work with them.

www.kidsource.com/NICHCY/learning_disabilities.html

This *KidSource* Web page offers general information about learning disabilities and a list of general suggestions for teachers.

Piaget, Jean

www.ship.edu/~cgboeree/piaget.html
www.funderstanding.com/piaget.cfm

Both of these Web sites provide information about Jean Piaget, including his biography and a summary of his major theories relating to the cognitive development of children.

Professional Ethics

www.nea.org/code.html

The National Education Association (NEA) provides a code of ethics for all teachers to follow.

Student Motivation

www.ericfacility.net/databases/ERIC_Digests/ed370200.html
www.kidsource.com/kidsource/content2/Student_Motivation.html
www.wpi.edu/Academics/CEDTA/ISG501/motivation.html

All teachers struggle with motivating their students to learn. These three Web sites offer basic information and definitions about student motivation, including the differences between intrinsic and extrinsic motivation and basic ways that teachers can motivate students to learn.

www.atozteacherstuff.com/tips/Motivating_Students/

This page from the *A to Z TeacherStuff* Web site provides tips from teachers to keep students motivated.

School Retention

www.drrobertbrooks.com/writings/articles/0211.html

This Web site provides a summary of research addressing the practice of retaining students who are failing in school. The summary notes that the practice is well researched, and many studies have discovered that not only does retention fail to improve achievement when compared to other remedial approaches but it also produces many adverse and unwanted effects for retained students.

PART II

THE PROCESS AND CONTENT OF REFLECTION

THREE

INTRODUCTION TO REFLECTIVE PROBLEM SOLVING

BEFORE READING CHAPTER 3—REFLECTIVE CONSIDERATIONS

- How do individuals become confident, professional teachers?
- How do professional teachers solve classroom problems?
- What are your beliefs about teaching?

> The field experience in this course has been a real learning experience for me. Nothing prepares you for the real world except firsthand experience. I thought that all students who entered the classroom would have a natural love of learning. Boy was I wrong! Some seem only to be in school because it's required. Education is not even on their priority list.

Many of you may agree with the sentiments of this prospective teacher who discovered during a field experience that teaching was not what she had expected. Both inexperienced and experienced teachers often report that they are overwhelmed by the educational problems that they face in classrooms. These problems range from students who are unmotivated and disconnected from the learning process to students who are years behind in their skills to students who are bored, angry, and disruptive in the classroom. With large numbers of students and pressure to cover an increasingly full curriculum, how can teachers cope with the complicated problems presented in the modern classroom? How can prospective teachers hope to gain the wisdom they need in order to become effective professionals?

In this chapter, this complex problem is explored as part of the journey prospective teachers take as they become educational professionals. According to researchers (Steffy, Wolfe, Pasch, & Enz, 2000), a professional teacher is one who is confident in his or her problem-solving abilities and is skillful in meeting the instructional needs of diverse groups of students. The most distinctive characteristic of the professional teacher is an overriding concern for the educational needs of students. In order to meet student needs, the professional teacher continuously seeks new learning and professional growth. The professional teacher is able to sort through a variety of classroom instructional options and has the skill and confidence to select those leading to the best options for a particular group of students (Steffy et al., 2000). While it is reasonable to expect that all teachers would want to be professional teachers—that is, teachers who ascertain what is best for students—this is not always the case. There are different instructional models that strive to achieve distinct educational goals, and two of these models are contrasted in the next section.

TRANSMISSIONAL VERSUS CONSTRUCTIVIST VIEWS OF INSTRUCTION

Two opposing views of classroom instruction are the *transmissional* approach and the *constructivist* approach (Lieberman, 1995; Null, 2004; Posner, 1998; Raines & Shadiow, 1995). These different approaches to teaching and learning are compared here so that the reader will become more aware of their distinctions and be able to determine the type of teacher they want to become.

The transmissional approach to teaching describes instructional methods as a set of procedures that a teacher would precisely follow to unfailingly produce student learning (Smyth, 1989). Much of the instruction provided in textbooks is of this type (Leu & Kinzer, 1995). In this approach, the teacher's manual provides directions about how to conduct the lesson, includes questions to ask students, and makes suggestions for student assignments and assessments. Transmission teachers rely extensively on textbook teaching to select instructional methods and materials for their students (Ben-Peretz, 1990). Unfortunately, by relying so much on the textbook—by utilizing a "canned" instructional approach—teachers often fail to meet the unique needs of their students. What they do deliver are rote skills and static textbook information. To some extent, administrators and parents may support this type of teaching because they believe it ensures a consistent level of instruction from every teacher. In the past, this type of textbook instruction was termed "teacher proof." Many educators view "teacher-proof" curriculum as a grave insult to the professional teacher because it assumes that textbook writers are better judges of how to teach than the teacher who is standing before the students. The transmissional view also perceives the teacher as a kind of inert conduit for the flow of information from teacher to student. Transmissional teaching minimizes the individual needs, interests, and motivations of both teachers and students. It is based on an assumption that following cookbook classroom procedures ensures that all students will learn at a consistent and predetermined level.

Another view of instruction is that of the constructivist teacher, that is, a teacher who is a reflective problem solver. In the constructivist view, learners construct their own knowledge by searching for meaning through experiences about the world. Although a teacher can and should provide experience and guidance for students, all new knowledge is synthesized by the student to produce a unique understanding based on previous knowledge (Brooks & Brooks, 1993).

In this view, the professional judgment of the teacher is critical as he or she makes decisions in the classroom to design experiences that encourage student learning. Learning cannot be coerced from students but must be skillfully elicited. This type of teaching requires a skillful, intelligent, and sensitive teacher. It requires teachers to be reflective about the events of the classroom and carefully plan lessons based on what students currently know and what they need to learn to bring them to the next level in their development.

This reflective approach to teaching has its roots with John Dewey, one of the most important educational thinkers of this century. Dewey (1933) noted that reflective thinking frees teachers from blindly following classroom routines (textbook instruction) or from impulsive, impromptu classroom planning. We have just discussed the problems with transmissional textbook teaching, but impulsive teaching has even greater shortcomings. The impulsive teacher's lack of planning indicates a teacher who has more concern for self than what is best for students. That is, the impulsive teacher plans what is convenient, easy, or interesting to him or her rather than what is best for students. It is my guess that the reader has had more than one impulsive teacher in their educational career, and the chief complaint that students make about such instruction is that it is confusing, uneven, and not focused on the needs of the learner.

In another description of the constructivist teacher, a more contemporary researcher, Schon (1983, 1987), calls the reflective approach *reflection-in-action.* According to Schon, reflection-in-action is when professionals use their expert judgment to solve complex problems based on their extensive knowledge of content and familiarity with a situation. Schon investigated the manner in which professionals in many different fields solve problems. He interviewed architects, physicians, and even jazz musicians—all professionals who, like teachers, have complex problems to solve. He found that reflective professionals from diverse fields all solve problems using similar processes.

For teachers, the reflective view of instruction describes good teaching as a problem-solving approach where the teacher's classroom experiences, knowledge of content, and understanding of learning theory are considered in order to produce a learning environment unique to the needs of a particular group of learners. This description of the reflective teacher is similar to characteristics of the professional teacher as described by Steffy et al. (2000). One of the primary ways that a teacher develops into a professional is through the process of reflective problem solving as described by Dewey and Schon (Steffy et al., 2000).

In addition, whereas the transmissional teacher utilizes a textbook as the primary tool of instruction, the constructivist teacher uses a variety of instructional tools, including primary sources, the Internet, literature, cooperative learning, inquiry, and community resources, in order to create a classroom environment exciting to students and conducive to learning. The constructivist teacher's knowledge of the problem-solving process and experience with a particular group of students are the guides for creating instruction, not following a set of instructions from a textbook or deciding what to do on the spur of the moment.

To a great extent, the constructivist teacher even views content knowledge differently than does the transmissional teacher. The transmissional teacher views knowledge as static, unchanging, and determined by authority figures. The reflective teacher views content knowledge as dynamic and ever changing as it is interpreted and constructed by the learner (King & Kitchener, 1994). For the constructivist teacher, this view of knowledge as dynamic creates the need for the teacher to utilize dynamic instructional methods and primary materials. For the constructivist teacher, science is taught as a changing field where scientists modify scientific theory based on new evidence derived from research. Knowledge is viewed as a dynamic when different perspectives are considered in a revision of historical events. Knowledge is viewed as a dynamic when language is viewed as a living entity that changes with the addition of international and technical terminology, slang, and definitions based on changes of usage within the culture.

The transmissional view of knowledge expects that science will be taught from textbooks, delivered by authority experts, and memorized by students. History is told from one dominant perspective, and language is taught as a set of grammar and spelling rules to be duplicated unfailingly in student writing.

The view of knowledge as static gives the transmissional teacher permission to use textbooks as a sole source of information to be memorized and reproduced by students on objective tests. It is the "old bones to old bones" perspective, where static knowledge in books is transferred into static knowledge held by students, without the need for a student's brain to be engaged in any manner. Hence, the use of the term transmissional teaching, that is, teaching where the chief objective is to transfer knowledge from teacher to student.

The dynamic view of knowledge requires that students interact with knowledge from books and others sources to analyze, synthesize, and evaluate what they learn and determine what that knowledge means to both them and their community. The role of the students is to construct their own understanding of knowledge rather than have it preprocessed and delivered to them via textbooks and teachers. The constructivist teacher engages in teaching and learning as a dynamic process that requires problem solving and reflection about what happened in the classroom and where instruction will take students next. The constructivist way of teaching is more difficult to achieve but a more exciting and engaging way to teach and interact with students.

BECOMING A REFLECTIVE PROBLEM SOLVER

Now let's talk about what this means to you as a teacher. Many education students relate (or complain) that their education instructors require reflection as a regular part of course activities. This reflection takes place in field experiences or during course assignments. Sometimes education students respond to reflective tasks like the following student.

> As a student at——College we had to do a lot of reflection. I didn't think we were really taught how to do it though. During field experiences we kept a reflective journal. I think many people just described their day.

You may feel like this student, who is willing to reflect about course activities and classroom events but who is confused about what the instructor wants and unsure about how to reflect and what reflection accomplishes. It would seem that good teaching should just simply "flow" from someone who wants to be a teacher and loves to work with children. The reflective writing required in many education classes can feel like "busy work" that takes time but doesn't help in the real classroom. How can reflection help teachers know what to do when working with students?

The argument made for the importance of reflection, according to Dewey, was to give a subject "serious and consecutive consideration," that is, thinking matters over carefully (1933, p. 3). It also means taking into consideration multiple factors when making complex decisions. Teachers make dozens of instructional decisions every day. A teacher who treats instructional decisions in a simple manner without consideration of these multiple factors is either a transmissional or impulsive teacher. The reflective teacher is one who considers the complexity of student problems and then carefully develops a solution to address that problem.

Another way to look at this is to consider that some individuals seem to benefit more from life experiences than others. We all know friends who make the same obvious mistakes over and over: someone who repeatedly loses jobs or who dates inappropriate people. This same pattern can be observed in teachers who repeat teaching behaviors that fail to help students to learn. You have probably had more than one of those teachers. Posner (1989) explained this by arguing that experience with no reflection leads to superficial and poor problem solving. As learners, we have all suffered in classrooms with teachers who have spent years in the classroom, yet we know they are poor teachers. For those teachers, years of experience and the evidence of poor results has not taught them how to improve their teaching. Obviously, while experience is important, it is not the complete answer.

Posner (1989) also claimed that reflection with no experience is not realistic and generally leads to unworkable solutions. That is, developing solutions to classroom problems while lacking experience with real students in real classrooms is ineffective. This is because educational problem solving requires practical solutions to problems that will work with specific learners. When a student is not learning, a solution must be found to quickly help the student. Untried theory is an academic game that experienced teachers view as futile and ineffective. Most students can recall a university instructor who had "book knowledge" about learning theory but who was not effective in teaching their own course. Education students often criticize their professors for being impractical and out of touch with "real" classrooms.

Most students have had firsthand experience with both of these teacher types as learners, and this should be convincing evidence that neither experience nor reflection alone can produce a good teacher. According to Posner (1989, p. 21), it is the combination of experience and reflection that produces growth and development as a teacher:

Experience + Reflection = Growth as a Teacher

MORE CHARACTERISTICS OF REFLECTIVE PROBLEM SOLVERS

> Reflection used to be a burden to me. I actually made up half of them my freshman year. Now that I am reflecting for a true purpose, I find it very helpful. Reflecting on my assignments helps me to critique my ideas and activities.

Researchers who have studied how reflective teachers and nonreflective teachers solve problems have divided the problem-solving process into four stages (Ferry & Ross-Gordon, 1998). The process begins when a teacher first identifies that a problem exists and moves to the final stage where the solution is reviewed and the teacher decides if the problem has been solved to his or her satisfaction. Researchers have found obvious differences between reflective and nonreflective teachers in the quality of the decision making at each stage of problem solving (Ferry & Ross-Gordon, 1998). We can examine the difference in reflective and non-reflective problem solving by considering a typical classroom problem.

All teachers have problems with students who shout out the answer to a question without waiting to be called on by the teacher. A nonreflective teacher might solve this problem by simply writing the name of the student on the board or by yelling at the student. For a nonreflective teacher, calling out answers might simply be viewed as a violation of classroom rules, whereas a reflective teacher might look at the problem as being more complex. One aspect to consider is the instructional results of calling out answers. Students who impulsively call out answers are not taking the time to develop a thoughtful response to the teacher's question. They might be shouting out the answer that they think the teacher wants to hear in order to move the lesson along or answering just to gain the teacher's attention. A reflective teacher wants students to become good thinkers and problem solvers; he or she would help students slow down their responses by encouraging them to think before they attempt to answer the question. To do this, the reflective teacher would provide "wait time" after asking a question so that students are given time to provide a thoughtful response. The teacher might tell the students to keep all hands down until everyone has thought of an answer. Research has shown that wait time encourages longer and more complex answers to questions (Rowe, 1986). The reflective teacher would also want to encourage respect for all students in the classroom by providing time for everyone to have a chance to answer—not just the fastest and the loudest students.

The description of the thinking processes of reflective and nonreflective teachers illustrates the differences in the problem-solving approaches of these two types of teachers. The nonreflective teacher looks for a fast, simple solution to the most obvious aspect of the problem—calling out answers. The reflective teacher considers the implications of the "calling out" behavior in relationship to the type of instructional response she wants to encourage in her students. The reflective teacher models the instructional behavior she wants to encourage in students by using wait time to achieve more thoughtful responses. The teacher facilitates this by asking the students to put down their hands and think carefully about their answer before the teacher calls on a student. The nonreflective teacher is simply attempting to make student behavior more manageable.

Recall the case study about Amy in the last chapter who was facing her first classroom crisis as a student teacher. Amy had not yet learned to be reflective and as a result was unable to come to grips with the first step in the problem-solving process: identifying the problem. As a first step in becoming a reflective teacher, Amy will need to learn to sort through the issues of her problem, including her responsibility in managing the lesson. If she engages in this problem-solving process, she will determine what she is responsible for, what she is able to change, and what is out of her direct control. If she can identify elements in her behavior she can change that will impact student behavior, Amy will be on her way to becoming a reflective problem solver.

If she continues to simply blame students and not acknowledge the necessity of changing how she interacts with them, we can predict that she will remain lost in self-recrimination and helplessness, leading to reproach from the students, her cooperating teacher, and her university supervisor. Many new teachers, including me, have been in that terrible, lost place where Amy finds herself. Recognizing these situations through the case studies provided in this book will hopefully allow the reader to spend less time in unproductive limbo and more time in reflective problem solving.

This book challenges prospective teachers to become reflective problem solvers and provides practice in the use of the reflective approach. The type of instruction advocated here is neither the simplest to understand nor the easiest to plan. It is easy to open up a textbook each day and simply follow the directions without a thought. The methods advocated here are sophisticated and are based on the assumption that prospective teachers want to become thoughtful, intelligent professionals who take their responsibility seriously in ensuring that children learn. Hopefully, you will develop a vision of yourself as this type of teacher as you work through the case studies and exercises presented here.

The final activity in this chapter will help you to continue your journey in becoming a reflective teacher and to identify the type of teacher you admire. This will help you to recognize the teaching characteristics you value. This is a reflective process and so may not seem particularly relevant to knowledge needed to become a teacher. At this point you might be more interested in learning how to write lesson plans or what behavior to expect from students of a given age. But you should know that the person you are now—with all of your beliefs, theories, and values about life—forms the foundation for the teacher you will become: understanding who you are now will help you make more reflective decisions about how to develop into the type of teacher you ultimately want to become.

END-OF-THE-CHAPTER ACTIVITY

The following strategy is designed to encourage you to examine your current theories and beliefs about learning. This is the first step to becoming a thoughtful, reflective teacher. The strategy is designed to reveal personal beliefs that have developed over a lifetime of schooling and to allow you to critique these beliefs and either affirm or discard them.

AFTER READING CHAPTER 3—PERSONAL BELIEFS STRATEGY

1. What were the characteristics of your best, most memorable teacher? Describe this teacher and what he or she did that affirmed you as a learner. How did you feel in that classroom? What did you learn and why was it important to you?

2. The characteristics you listed about your best teacher in Question 1 reflect your personal beliefs about what makes a good teacher. Read your answer again and list 10 characteristics or qualities that describe that teacher.

1. ______________________________

____

2. ______________________________

____

3. ______________________________

____

4. ______________________________

____

5. ______________________________

____

6. ______________________________

____

7. ______________________________

____

8. ______________________________

____

9. ______________________________

____

10. ____

____

REFERENCES

Ben-Peretz, M. (1990). *The teacher-curriculum encounter: Freeing teachers from the tyranny of texts.* New York: State University of New York Press.

Brooks, J. G., & Brooks, M. G. (1993). *In search of understanding: The case for constructivist classrooms.* Alexandria, VA: Association for Supervision and Curriculum Development.

Dewey, J. (1933). *How we think.* Lexington, MA: D. C. Heath.

Ferry, N. M., & Ross-Gordon, J. M. (1998). An inquiry into Schon's epistemology of practice: Exploring links between experience and reflective practice. *Adult Education Quarterly, 48*(2), 98–112.

King, P. M., & Kitchener, K. S. (1994). *Developing reflective judgment.* San Francisco: Jossey-Bass.

Leu, D., & Kinzer, C. (1995). *Effective reading instruction.* Englewood Cliffs, NJ: Merrill Prentice Hall.

Lieberman, A. (1995). Practices that support teacher development: Transforming conceptions of professional learning. *Phi Delta Kappan, 76*(8), 591–596.

Null, J. W. (2004). Is constructivism traditional? Historical and practical perspectives on a popular advocacy. *The Educational Forum, 68*(2), 180–188.

Posner, G. J. (1989). *Field experience.* New York: Longman.

Raines, P., & Shadiow, L. (1995). Reflection and teaching: The challenge of thinking beyond the doing. *The Clearing House, 68*(4), 271–274.

Rowe, M. B. (1986). Wait time: Slowing down may be a way of speeding up! *Journal of Teacher Education, 37*(1), 43–50.

Schon, D. A. (1983). *The reflective practitioner.* New York: Basic Books.

Schon, D. A. (1987). *Educating the reflective practitioner.* San Francisco: Jossey-Bass.

Smyth, J. (1989). Developing and sustaining critical reflection in teacher education. *Journal of Teacher Education, 40*(2), 2–9.

Steffy, B. E., Wolfe, M. P., Pasch, S. H., & Enz, B. J. (2000). *Life cycle of the career teacher.* Thousand Oaks, CA: Corwin Press.

INTERNET RESOURCES

Constructivism

http://carbon.cudenver.edu/~mryder/itc_data/constructivism.html
www.funderstanding.com/constructivism.cfm

These two sites include a variety of resources describing and defining constructivism and its theorists.

www.towson.edu/csme/mctp/Essays.html

This site has a long list of essays and papers that describe constructivism.

Dewey, John

www.molloy.edu/academic/philosophy/sophia/TOPICS/phiedu/contents.htm

This site provides an online collection of the writings of great Western philosophers including John Dewey.

Reflection

http://alex.edfac.usyd.edu.au/LocalResource/Study1/hattonart.html
www.findarticles.com/cf_dls/m0NQM/3_42/108442653/p1/article.jhtml
http://teachers.net/gazette/MAY01/marshall.html
www.cotf.edu/ete/teacher/reflect.html

Here you will find a selection of articles and sites that describe and discuss teacher reflection. They provide a variety of perspectives on teacher reflection that supplements the chapter discussion.

Wait Time

www.ericfacility.net/databases/ERIC_Digests/ed370885.html
www.mdk12.org/instruction/success_mspap/general/projectbetter/thinkingskills/ts-83–85.html

These two articles describe wait time and its importance and how it can improve the quality of classroom discussions. These benefits include increasing the number and type of students responding to the teacher's questions and increasing the number, length, and complexity of student responses.

FOUR

DEVELOPING AN EDUCATIONAL PHILOSOPHY

BEFORE READING CHAPTER 4—REFLECTIVE CONSIDERATION ON DEVELOPING A PHILOSOPHY OF EDUCATION

- What is a philosophy of teaching?
- What does a philosophy include?
- Why do I need an educational philosophy?
- How do I develop one?

In this chapter we will examine the idea of a philosophy of education and what developing a philosophy can bring to the reflective process for you as a teacher. This philosophy will be used in Chapters 5, 6, and 7, where you will analyze and make decisions about the case study problems. Remember, the case studies serve as a virtual context to explore common classroom issues such as discipline, student motivation, and the special needs of students. The ideas in this chapter will teach you about and prepare you to use an educational philosophy that can be used for reflective problem solving.

WHY WRITE A PHILOSOPHY OF EDUCATION?

> Completing a traditional program of teacher education as preparation for working in [the] emotional cauldron [of schools] is like preparing to swim

> the English Channel by doing laps in the university pool. Swimming is not swimming. Having a warm shower, a clean towel, a private locker, your own lane, and a heated, guarded chlorinated pool has nothing whatever to do with the grueling realities of eight-foot swells of freezing water for 22 miles without being certain of your direction. (Haberman, 1995, p. 2)

In the above quote, Martin Haberman compares the sheltered experience of a teacher education program housed at a college or university to the harsh realities of working in schools. Many new teachers report that their teacher education program did not prepare them to deal with the complex issues and student problems they experienced during student teaching or in their first positions as teachers (Lortie, 1975). This chapter is designed to do that by providing tools to help new teachers survive their first year and continue to grow throughout their careers.

To continue with Haberman's metaphor, the way to succeed in teaching is to have tools that will keep you afloat in any water, in any weather. What are those tools according to the metaphor? When new teachers are struggling in the classroom, they often will seek simple solutions to solve complex problems. If a teacher can't get students quickly settled and prepared to learn, they may use small techniques to help make that happen. The reality is that small techniques, such as promising students a popcorn party or putting their names on the board to punish them, is like a swimmer using a colorful floatie or a life preserver to travel through Haberman's 8-foot swells of icy water. These techniques might seem effective and they might provide a little confidence, but swimmers can easily get tumbled by the swell. These temporary solutions will never adequately address pervasive classroom problems. Clearly, the teacher needs more than a rubber orca toy for the times when the classroom seas are rough. What teachers really need are an excellent set of muscles and a swimming technique that will last a lifetime. Building a swimmer's body will truly solve the problem of keeping the teacher afloat under his or her own power no matter what the seas of education present. This chapter will examine concepts that will build long-term capacity for classroom problem solving. These capacity builders help teachers think through complex problems and develop strategies to solve them. Examples of these muscle builders are pedagogy, content knowledge, and classroom experience—all components that contribute to a philosophy of education.

Many of you may view an educational philosophy as something you write for an education class or something you might dust off to prepare for an interview, but it is much more than that. An educational philosophy consists of many parts, but the most important elements are your own deep-rooted beliefs, values, and attitudes about children and learning. These might include the belief that all children are able to learn (no matter their abilities or current skill levels) or the belief that children should be motivated to learn by using exciting, hands-on activities that directly address their needs and interests. Your beliefs and attitudes about learning will direct your professional growth and affect your behavior in the classroom—whether you are aware of these beliefs or not (Richardson, 1996).

In Chapter 3, we explored a special type of thinking called reflection. In this chapter we will explore how to use reflection to develop a philosophy of education. Reflection is the process of *how* to think—it is a verb. Educational philosophy is *what* the teacher considers during reflection—it is a noun. Both ways of using reflection—verb and noun—are essential for the design of good teaching.

Most prospective teachers express a sense of mission to teach because they have an affinity for children or young people, and they want to act on that feeling by positively influencing the lives of students. No one goes into teaching to be the horrible teacher we all remember who terrorized students or who bored them to death. We all want to communicate our dedication to good teaching so that others will be inspired to learn. An educational philosophy will help you better understand yourself as a teacher and communicate your special teaching dedication to students and others.

Developing an educational philosophy takes time, experience, and reflection. With an increased awareness of yourself as a teacher and the type of educational philosophy your beliefs represent, you can begin to make your ideals and beliefs a reality for your students. A philosophy is only as good as the extent to which it has a positive impact on students. So, as a prospective teacher, now is the time to begin developing your philosophy. This chapter will help you do that by providing background knowledge and exercises to help you define your personal educational philosophy.

EDUCATIONAL PHILOSOPHY AND CLASSROOM EXPERIENCE

Shulman (1986) described several types of teacher knowledge. These included knowledge of teaching practices—how to teach and knowledge of content—and what to teach. The model in Figure 4.1 illustrates the components of a

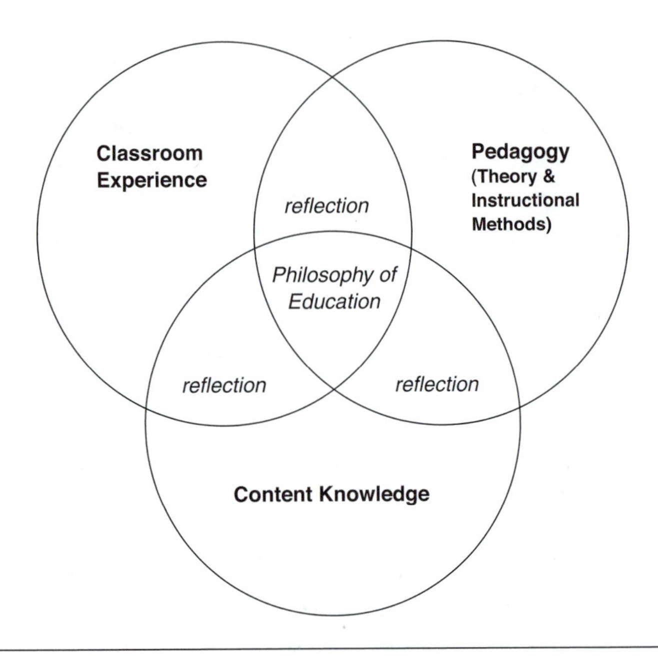

Figure 4.1 Components of a Philosophy of Education

philosophy of education and how reflection links the components together. One of the model components, *classroom experience,* represents firsthand experience working in a classroom. One reason why it is difficult for new teachers to be highly effective in the classroom is their lack of experience. A talented new teacher may have extensive knowledge of content and a comprehensive knowledge of teaching theory but still lack the classroom experience needed to fuse this knowledge to practical classroom activities.

For example, a teacher may have vast knowledge of animal anatomy and a wonderful lesson plan, but unless the teacher also understands how to organize lab materials and how to set standards for student behavior and safety, a dissection lesson could turn into a smelly free-for-all. The practical knowledge gained from classroom experience includes understanding student behavior and capabilities and the appropriate expectations for students at different age levels. It also includes classroom management issues, such as dealing with materials, student movement, and lesson transitions. Most importantly, it includes developing a classroom climate that leads to student learning: a climate that addresses the physical, cultural, and social needs of diverse groups of students. Sometimes this is also referred to as classroom context (Fullan,

2003), that is, the special qualities that make each classroom unique, such as age, race, ethnicity, gender, degree of parental and community support, as well as all the qualities unique to a particular group of students in a particular school at a particular point in time.

Remember Amy, the student teacher from Chapter 2? Mr. Shannon, her cooperating teacher, described his class as one of the most difficult groups that he had taught. A seasoned teacher like Mr. Shannon can rely on past knowledge to anticipate what to expect and determine what to do; nevertheless, the vast range of possibilities in human behavior can present unanticipated outcomes that bewilder even the most experienced professional. A teacher needs to simultaneously consider both the ordinary and the unique features of a particular group of students in order to know what to commonly expect in addition to calling upon experience to decide how to deal with the unexpected.

The model in Figure 4.1 is represented with overlapping circles because all of the model's components interact to produce an integrated philosophy of education. Classroom experience, content knowledge, and pedagogy all interact and are necessary for effective teaching. Without classroom experience, it is difficult for a teacher to anticipate what a group of students need; without pedagogy, the teacher cannot develop an effective plan for teaching; and without content knowledge, what would be taught?

EDUCATIONAL PHILOSOPHY AND PEDAGOGY

This takes us to the next component of the model, which is pedagogy. Pedagogy is usually defined as the science of teaching. In the current most useful understanding of pedagogy, both educational theory and instructional methods are considered essential. Instructional methods are the specific strategies and techniques that teachers use during teaching. For example, cooperative learning, inquiry, lecture, learning centers, and the use of advanced organizers are all considered instructional methods. Instructional methods are not addressed in detail here because this topic is usually covered extensively during methods courses in most programs. However, theories of learning and motivation will be addressed in this chapter because knowledge of theory is increasingly viewed as an important element for developing good teaching. In addition, educational theory is included on teacher competency exams such as the PRAXIS. In order to obtain the highest scoring level for the PRAXIS exams, when analyzing educational problems, answers must be supported by theory and educational research. Not only is educational theory needed to pass exams, but more importantly, it is a tool that allows teachers to generate specific solutions to solve the classroom problems that all teachers will encounter. Theory is an abstract concept; therefore, it is important to think about what is meant by the word *theory* and how it applies to teaching.

Learning theories are assumptions or predictions about how and why individuals learn. These assumptions are tested through research to find out how true they are. After a theory has been researched and determined to be potentially successful, teachers can consider using these generalizations about learning during reflective problem solving. Using knowledge that others have generated about the best ways to teach provides guidance about what teachers might try when they are attempting to solve a difficult classroom problem (Brophy & Good, 1986; Friedman & Fisher, 1998; Marzano, Pickering & Pollock, 2001). If teachers do not utilize research or learning theory, they are compelled to rely on trial-and-error problem solving, a lengthy process that delays finding solutions for their students.

Learning theory provides answers to critical questions, explaining why students are motivated to learn and how new learning is integrated into students' existing knowledge. (Don't you agree that all learners deserve timely and informed solutions to their learning problems?) At the end of the chapter are a list of Web sites that describe effective teaching practices and what works in classrooms.

There are many different learning theories, and it is important for teachers to understand their own personal theories of learning because, as stated earlier, research has shown that these greatly influence the classroom decisions that teachers make—even if the teacher is unaware of his or her personal theories as such (Richardson, 1996). The theories of learning that prospective teachers bring to the classroom are primarily based on their own experiences as learners and, as a result, are largely retained even as prospective teachers move through a teacher education program and take charge of their own classrooms (Lortie, 1975).

Often, teachers claim that theory is not practical. Some teachers say that the theories they learned in their university courses do not work in real classrooms. When teachers talk about theory in this manner, they are often describing the theories studied from textbooks, which they have memorized for tests but have not internalized for their own teaching. Naturally, a theory is not useful if it is not a part of the teacher's belief system or if the teacher doesn't use it to make decisions about the classroom. The practical reason for understanding learning theory is to enable teachers to use it to influence daily decisions in the classroom.

Everyone has theories about learning, even if you can't name one right now. For example, the concept that very young children learn best through hands-on activities rather than by recitation of material is a theory of learning held by many. In past centuries, it was not recognized that the thinking of small children was different from that of adults, and very young children were taught in the same manner as adults. Children were required to memorize information and recite it as proof of learning, even if they were unable to understand the content. For example, young children might recite the Declaration of Independence or the Bible. Many theorists, including Piaget, carefully observed and documented how young children understand the world. Through research like Piaget's (1966), theorists have dispelled the theory, or belief, that the thinking processes of children and adults are the same. They determined that the language and ideas expressed in the Declaration of Independence, and much of the Bible, were too complex for young children to understand. Most early childhood teachers share this belief and organize their instruction according to these researched-based theories. You may also know of parents who understand developmental learning theory. Many parents select toys that are developmentally appropriate to help their children to learn basic skills such as colors, letters, and numbers.

Why is learning theory an important part of a teacher's educational philosophy? According to researchers, teachers who use theory to guide their practices are more deliberate and thoughtful classroom problem solvers (Bigge & Shermis, 1999; Eisner, 1985; Leu & Kinzer, 1995; Shulman, 1986; Weaver, 1990). Researchers reason that teachers who are able to explain and defend their instructional methods are better teachers (Haberman, 1995). If teachers can explain how and why they act, they are more focused in their instruction and more likely to accomplish instructional goals. The students of such teachers learn more because the teacher is focused and organized and can better plan what he or she wants to accomplish. The alternative to theory-based teaching is impulsive teaching, that is, when the teacher randomly decides each day what to do, or teachers who work directly from a textbook. We discussed both of these types of teachers in the last chapter. The first type of teacher is confusing to students, and the second is boring.

The use of theory, in practical terms, offers teachers generalized solutions to common classroom problems. The solutions provided by theories, while they cannot be applied in a generalized, careless manner, offer teachers a variety of researched-based solutions. The development of a personalized theory system provides teachers a filter, or lens, to consider the merits of various solutions before they are selected or rejected. For example, motivating children to read is a common classroom problem. Different theories offer different solutions to solve this problem. Behavior theory advocates rewarding the child with praise or privileges. Self-determination theory advocates providing interesting books, a varied literacy curriculum, and a teacher who models a love of literature (Brophy, 1998).

Which is the better theory, and which provides the best solution to the problem? That depends on the teacher's interpretation of what motivates children to read—is it rewards, such as pizza, or good literature? A good theory is one that provides the best answers to the teacher's classroom problems and provides a good match to the teacher's underlying beliefs about how and why children learn. The behaviorist teacher believes that all motivation is external to children, that self-motivation does not exist. The goals theory teacher believes that all children have an innate desire and curiosity to learn and will do so if a supportive environment is provided. These are very different belief systems—which do you believe?

Maslow's Hierarchy of Needs

What are some helpful theories for prospective teachers to consider? Let's take a closer look at some theories that teachers have found particularly useful. What follows is certainly not all the theories that a teacher may use to explain classroom problems. These are just a sampling of theories that teachers seem to find particularly easy to understand and apply to the classroom. Many teachers find Maslow's hierarchy (1968) a helpful theory because it provides a good explanation for why some children are able to learn and others are not (Figure 4.2). Remember the story of Jennifer at the beginning of the book? How could a teacher explain why a student who had been successful in school suddenly stops learning? And how would the teacher explain why the student started learning again? Maslow's hierarchy explains Jennifer's situation and the situation of many students who, like Jennifer, face stressful life situations. Consider Figure 4.2, and notice that learning is placed at a high level in the hierarchy of needs at Level 5, Cognitive Needs. Maslow's theory states that all lower level needs have to be met before higher level needs can

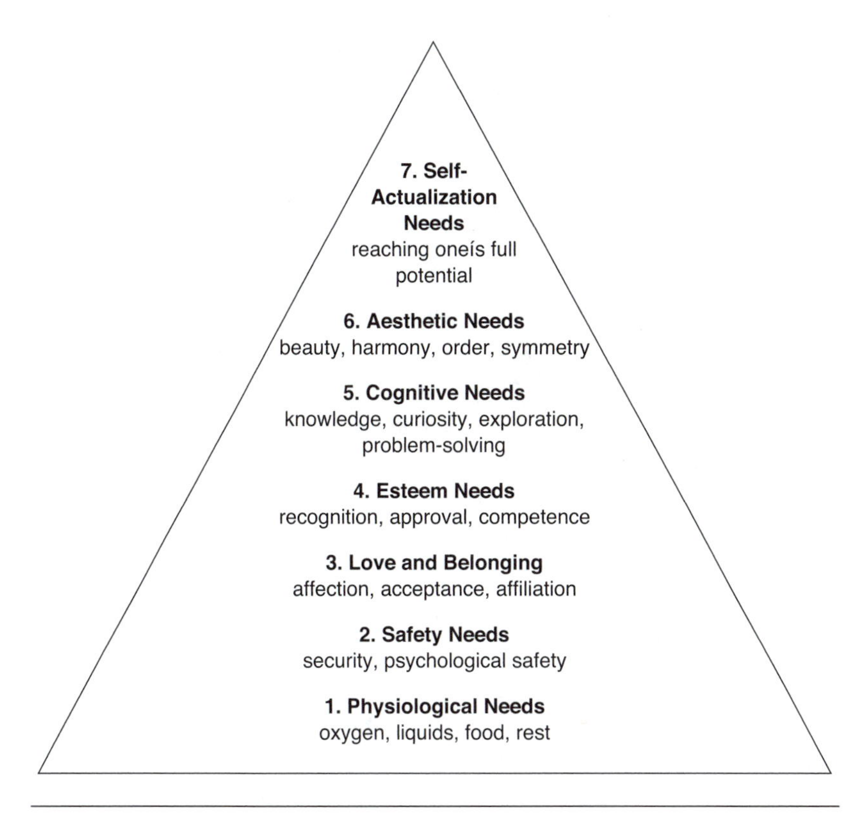

Figure 4.2 Maslow's Hierarchy

be fulfilled. This means that, in order to learn, students must be fed and clothed, and they must have enough sleep. They must also feel safe, secure, loved, and accepted in both their home and school environments. Last, they must believe they are capable of doing the work at school that is required of them. How many children in our society live in unhappy or even dangerous homes? How many children experience divorce, a family death, or frequent moves where they must adjust to new schools and friends? These are common life events, but according to Maslow's theory, these events may interrupt or stop the learning process. With respect to the school environment, how many children feel unaccepted at school and face teasing and isolation by their classmates? How many children are behind in their learning and struggle each day to be successful and feel competent? Maslow's theory predicts that children with unfulfilled social or instructional needs will have a difficult time achieving.

According to the hierarchy, the needs of the physical body must be satisfied first, and then social and emotional needs must be fulfilled before a student is ready and able to learn. In our turbulent society, sometimes parents have difficulty providing for all of their children's needs, which explains why schools now take a greater role in providing for children. These days, not only is lunch served but breakfast and after-school programs provide snacks to make sure students are well nourished. Many schools have family centers to clothe children and provide for other basic material needs. Schools offer screenings for hearing, exams for eyes, and dental check-ups, all in an effort to support the physical needs of the child. Still, all of these services may not be enough for some children. As a teacher you will have to recognize when outside services and resources should be alerted to help an unsupported, neglected, or abused child. Teachers who understand Maslow's theory are sensitive to the needs of children and attempt to investigate and determine why a child is not learning.

In the case of Jennifer, a change in her home life, a new father, seemed to challenge her sense of security and safety. Her ability to learn was disrupted until she was able to regain her sense of security and safety within the circle of her new family. After making that adjustment, Jennifer was able to start learning again. As her teacher, I did little more to help Jennifer than be supportive and communicate with her family about the changes she was facing. In this case it was enough that I understood what was occurring in Jennifer's life. In other cases, a teacher might need to intervene with resources and support services to help the student and the family.

Self-Determination Theory

This may make you begin to feel that your job as teacher is impossible. How can your students learn when learning is not supported at home? Many teachers admit this frustration about teaching, but another theory, *self-determination theory,* explains what a teacher can do to create a classroom environment where students are able to learn. Many teachers like this theory because it has only three components for them to consider when they are creating a classroom environment or developing lessons and activities. Self-determination theory specifies that the classroom learning environment must satisfy three student needs (Deci & Ryan, 1998). These are

Competence—developing and exercising learning skills

Relatedness—affiliation with others through prosocial relationships

Autonomy—self-determination in deciding what to do and how to do it

The first principle, *competence,* means that students should be taught at an appropriate level for each individual. School assignments should not be so difficult as to frustrate the learner, but not so easy as to be boring. Although this seems an easy and obvious principle to follow, it can be extremely challenging when students are at many different levels of instruction. It is estimated that in the average classroom students range from two grade levels below to two grade levels above the grade of the classroom. To be effective with so many instructional levels, teachers need to utilize good assessment techniques so they can determine the appropriate level to present lessons.

Teachers who present information straight from the textbook were mentioned earlier in the chapter. These textbook teachers are not addressing the range of student abilities with their "one size fits all" lessons. Naturally, some students will be frustrated if they cannot learn as fast as other students. When they sense they are falling behind, they begin to question their competence, according to Maslow's hierarchy of needs. If this continues, the student may stop trying and fall still further behind. Teachers must develop lessons that support students' competency to learn because this will sustain students' motivation to learn. At the other end of the range, if the teacher fails to provide lessons for students who are achieving at higher levels, these students may also stop learning. Often, academically talented students already know the material being presented. Over time they may become bored with school and disengage from the learning process.

Some of you are no doubt bright students who experienced boring classrooms and teachers. The textbook teacher presents lessons to address the average level of the classroom. This neglects the needs of lower- and higher-achieving students. Is that fair? Don't all children deserve a chance to be both successful and challenged in school?

The second principle, called *relatedness,* means that students need to feel they are liked and accepted by the teacher and the other students. According to this theory, it is the responsibility of the teacher to develop a classroom climate of acceptance and respect for all students. Often students follow the teacher's lead and treat each other according to how the teacher behaves. Because of this, the teacher should not play favorites or ostracize certain students or certain groups of students. Although this may seem obvious—naturally a teacher should model fair and accepting behavior—it is harder to achieve than it seems. Some students are difficult, even unlikable, and their challenging behavior can wear down the patience of even the most compassionate teacher. A teacher who is impatient and negative toward a difficult student gives the other students in the classroom permission to treat that student in the same manner. Difficult students often become socially isolated. Soon they feel that not only have they displeased the teacher, but they also find they have no friends among their classmates. According to self-determination theory, this social isolation will have a negative effect on their learning. Recalling Maslow's hierarchy, in order to learn, a student must feel accepted and loved at home and at school.

Both Maslow's theory and self-determination theory identify social acceptance as a necessary foundation for learning. Now, is this true in every case of every student? Not necessarily; there may be students who learn in spite of terrible classroom environments and social isolation. No theory is correct 100% of the time; it wouldn't be a theory, then, it would be a certainty. Good theories provide teachers generalizations that work more often than not. In the case of relatedness, most of us would agree that we learn better in an environment where we feel accepted and where our ideas are valued.

Race and class are special cases where teachers need to be especially vigilant about their own behavior and how students treat each other. This is particularly true of minority students. The majority of teachers in this county come from white, middle-class backgrounds. Many of us experienced a racist upbringing even if it didn't seem so at the time. All teachers must examine their classroom behavior and attitudes toward students who are different from themselves to ensure that they are not being biased. It is easy to fall into the trap of believing that a child who lives in a trailer home or public housing cannot learn as well as those from middle-class backgrounds. We will review case studies of minority and special needs students to help us to examine our possible (and likely) ingrained biases toward students who are "different."

The last principle of self-determination theory is *autonomy.* Autonomy means that students need a sense of control over their learning and choices in their activities. The idea of student autonomy is controversial. Teachers often object to the notion of student choice, arguing that students do not have the necessary judgment needed to determine what they should learn. They claim it is the responsibility of the teacher and school to determine what students need academically. Also student choice can be difficult for teachers to manage when the curriculum is filled with state and local mandates. Many teachers feel they don't have enough time to accomplish what is required, much less give students choices in topics and activities. To explore this common teacher dilemma, we will examine cases in which teachers face conflict about what they desire to teach and what they are required to teach.

Countering these arguments, the self-determination theorist would say that, although no one would claim that students should have complete control over their learning, appropriate student choice based on the student's age and maturity is critically important. Younger students should have less freedom than older students, but some choice is important for everyone. Students greatly appreciate even small choices in activities, such as selecting their own writing or research topics or selecting the book they want to read during silent reading time.

In self-determination theory, intrinsic or internal motivation is deemed essential. To state it simply, if students only learn when outside forces compel them do so, what happens to learning when those forces are no longer present? If students only read when rewarded with pizza, if they only study to earn a grade, if they only behave well to avoid consequences (punishment), will they ever develop the desire for these outcomes without reinforcement or coercion? Some theorists fear that they won't (Kohn, 1993), and they point to students who never read a book outside of school, who won't try to learn unless they are assured of a high grade, and who won't act in an appropriate manner unless a tangible reward is attached. The practice of rewarding students, so common in today's schools, is fatiguing for teachers and may undermine the internal reasons students have for desiring these things for themselves—a love of reading, a passion to learn, or a desire to contribute to a harmonious classroom. This brings us back to the principle of autonomy and to the consideration that if we want students to exercise judgment in making appropriate choices, exhibit self-control in their behavior, and demonstrate internal motivation to learn, how they will learn to do so? In a classroom strictly controlled by the teacher, if the student has no opportunity to develop or exercise these behaviors in school, how will these be maintained later in life?

Recalling the case study of Hannah from Chapter 2, it appeared that Hannah had a motivation problem, because when tested she was found to be academically capable. Let's examine Hannah's behavior according to self-determination theory to see if that theory can help explain Hannah's problem. To effect this, Hannah's teacher, Mrs. Weinstock, would first review the three student needs described by self-determination theory—competence, relatedness, and autonomy—to ascertain if the classroom learning environment was satisfying these needs for Hannah.

To address competence, Mrs. Weinstock would first make sure that all the assignments made for Hannah were at the appropriate level of skill. Hannah greatly needs to feel a sense of competence; she needs to feel confident and capable about her assignments because her refusal to try is based on the self-perception that her efforts only produce failure. Mrs. Weinstock should look at Hannah's test results and plan lessons at an appropriate level for Hannah and then provide supportive, objective, and encouraging feedback to Hannah about the results of her efforts. With regard to relatedness, based on the case study description, Hannah really needs a friend in Mrs. Weinstock's classroom. Although it is difficult for teachers to manipulate student interactions and friendships, Mrs. Weinstock should help Hannah mediate the social landscape of the fourth grade, because Hannah is shy and seems incapable of doing this for herself. Mrs. Weinstock needs to strongly advocate for Hannah with the other students and help her locate a few compatible buddies to provide support and friendship. It may be that the lack of social support for Hannah is the most harmful aspect of Mrs. Weinstock's classroom, and if Hannah felt even marginally secure and accepted, she would begin to learn even without prodding by her teacher. Last, self-determination theory advocates that students need some level of autonomy, or choice, over classroom assignments and activities. If Mrs. Weinstock provides limited choices based on Hannah's special interests, she may discover that Hannah does not require quite so much teacher urging. Patience and sustained effort are required from her teacher to implement this plan of specialized instruction and social support for Hannah because Hannah's motivation is so low that she appears to have withdrawn from the educational process. On the other hand, sometimes a withdrawn child will respond to a teacher with a minimum amount of intervention. I have known a difficult child to completely turn around for a teacher who simply granted the child 10 minutes of special computer time. Teachers with students like Hannah never know the result of their special intervention until they try.

Constructivism

The last theory that will be discussed is *constructivism.* Constructivism is a broad theory of learning widely advocated by educational experts. It is the theory embedded in the INTASC Teacher Standards (Darling-Hammond,

Transmissional Classrooms	*Constructivist Classrooms*
Behavioral psychology	Cognitive psychology
Curriculum is presented part to whole, with emphasis on basic skills.	Curriculum is presented whole to part, with emphasis on big concepts.
Curricular activities rely heavily on textbooks and workbooks.	Curricular activities rely heavily on primary sources and manipulation of data and materials.
Students practice skills and memorize information.	Students actively pursue learning and construct knowledge.
Students primarily work alone	Students primarily work in groups
Students are viewed as "blank slates" onto which information is transmitted by the teacher.	Students are viewed as thinkers with emerging theories about the world.
Teachers generally behave in a didactic manner, disseminating information to students.	Teachers generally behave in a dynamic manner, mediating the environment for students.
Teachers seek the correct answer to validate student learning of content knowledge and skills.	Teachers seek the students' point of view in order to understand students' views and develop ideas for use in future lessons.
Assessment of student learning is viewed entirely through testing.	Assessment of student learning is interwoven with observations of students at work and through student performance and portfolios.
Learning is expected to be uniform, the same for everyone.	Learning is expected to be individual, different for everyone.

Figure 4.3 Transmissional Versus Constructivist Classrooms

Source: Table adapted from Brooks & Brooks (1993), *In Search of Understanding: The Case for Constructivist Classrooms.* Alexandria, VA: Association for Supervision and Curriculum Development.

Wise, & Klein, 1995). These national standards are designed to guide teachers to be effective in the classroom. Currently, constructivist theory is in competition with another theory—the behaviorist or transmissional theory. See Figure 4.3 for a comparison of transmissional and constructivist theories (adapted from

Brooks & Brooks, 1993). Although it is somewhat controversial, constructivist theory is recommended as a better theory by many educational experts for its efficacy in creating democratic citizens. While problem solving and decision making are primary goals of constructivist theory, transmissional theory tends to promote conformity, compliance to authority, and passive learning.

PHILOSOPHY OF EDUCATION AND CONTENT KNOWLEDGE

Finally, the last component of our model is *content knowledge,* which is understanding the facts, information, skills, and organization of a given content area. This includes knowing the steps of multiple-digit multiplication, how clouds form, or how to support the writing of a thesis with examples and evidence. You should have learned most of your content knowledge in courses outside of your professional education courses. As the model in Figure 4.1 represents with the overlapping circles of theory, experience, and content, teachers have to learn how to present content knowledge in ways that students can understand. This means no longer viewing content from the perspective of a learner but from that of a teacher.

Therefore, with respect to teaching multiple-digit multiplication to third graders, teachers need to understand how a third grader thinks about math. According to Piaget, most third graders cannot use abstraction functions when they solve problems; therefore, children will need concrete models—base ten blocks or other physical models that represent the place value system. The principle is the same for all other content areas. To the surprise of many high school teachers, most adolescents are also unable to use abstraction to solve math and science problems. Most high school students also operate at a concrete level and therefore need materials and activities to demonstrate abstract concepts and processes (Dulit, 1972). For example, in a high school chemistry class, it would be helpful if students could build models of chemical compounds to explore how bonds function.

All teachers must understand the process of developmental thinking and their students' level of prior knowledge in order to design lessons appropriate for their level of comprehension. The teacher must provide a variety of examples, explanations, demonstrations, and hands-on activities that are best for demonstrating a concept or skill to a particular group of students at a particular age or level of skill (Shulman, 1986). Part of being an expert teacher is anticipating the kinds of questions students will ask, knowing what aspect of the content will be most difficult for students, and being ready with the best examples and demonstrations that will facilitate learning. The development of this knowledge naturally requires experience with students to observe what works and what doesn't work. It also requires generalizations—theories about what to anticipate for a certain grade level and understanding why a lesson worked or didn't work, based on the teacher's best insight about how students learn. We have returned again to the concept of theory, because, according to Figure 4.1, theory, experience, and content knowledge are synthesized in order for effective instruction to take place. Your understanding of the theories of child and adolescent development will, in most cases, be cultivated during your courses in child development and educational psychology.

END-OF-THE-CHAPTER ACTIVITY—DEVELOPING A PHILOSOPHY OF EDUCATION

Returning to the swimming metaphor, it is time to start developing the swimmer's body and the technique that will allow you to handle any oceanic mishap that your future students might throw your way. This begins with reflection about your personal theories of teaching, but it continues with consideration of what other teachers and educators have determined to be possible solutions to the classroom problems that all teachers face. Just as new training techniques have produced Olympic swimmers who can travel faster and endure longer distances, theory and research can produce teachers who understand more quickly and competently how to help students learn.

One of the most important purposes of reflective problem solving is to discover and examine current personal theories of teaching in relation to those advocated by educational experts, researchers, and theorists. The purpose of this activity is not to replace your existing beliefs developed through life experiences with new ideas from your educational studies but rather to integrate new educational ideas and theories with your personal beliefs. The reflective teacher reviews and evaluates his or her beliefs and ideas when confronted by new ideas and experiences and chooses to either affirm existing views or decide that the old beliefs are not appropriate and replace them with the new ones. Therefore, the teacher's personal beliefs are strengthened by an increased self-awareness while also being enriched by the ideas of others in the profession.

You can think of an educational philosophy as a kind of packaging for your beliefs to be presented to others. Educational philosophy asks and answers all the important questions about being an effective teacher. These questions are answered by your personal beliefs as informed by what you have learned about teaching and learning. Teachers continue to ask and answer these questions throughout their professional lives. The following activities, broken into four steps, will lead to a draft of a philosophy of education for you. The first step is a narrative of the different components of the philosophy of education. The next three steps will walk you through the process of completing each component by first brainstorming ideas and then developing a narrative from that list.

Step One—Own Values and Beliefs

Review what you wrote about your most memorable teacher from Chapter 3. List these qualities as a part of your philosophy, because they reflect your values and beliefs about what makes a good teacher. For example, these may indicate that you are a "caring teaching," that is, a teacher who is loving and nurturing to students. You could also state that you are a "competent teacher," that is, a teacher who understands the content knowledge that you will be responsible to teach. As an expert in a subject area such as science, history, or language arts you have obtained the knowledge to educate students about academics and help them become successful in life.

Review your most memorable teachers and list your values and beliefs about what makes a good teacher. From that list of values and beliefs, describe the type of teacher you will be:

A. List personal values and beliefs.

B. Develop a narrative describing your values and beliefs as a teacher.

Step Two—Classroom Experience

Actual classroom experience is often viewed by prospective teachers as one of the most important activities that create knowledgeable and confident teachers. In this step of philosophy development you should review every experience that may have contributed to your understanding of classroom teaching. These could include all your field and practicum experiences and substitute teaching, along with experiences such as coaching, teaching Bible school, counseling in a summer camp, or even baby-sitting. All of these interactions with children or adolescents will have contributed to your understanding of what to expect from various ages and grade levels. They will have also honed your communication skills in gaining and keeping students' attention along with providing information about the range of abilities and interests to expect from specific groups of students. Direct experience is a powerful teacher, and it is natural to turn to these direct experiences when you begin reviewing and analyzing case studies.

Review your current teaching experiences.

A. List all your teaching experiences.

B. Develop a narrative describing your experiences.

Step Three—Pedagogy

Adding knowledge of pedagogy to your existing value and belief system will make you a knowledgeable and reflective teacher. Your professional knowledge and content knowledge combined with experience about the practical aspects of the classroom will provide you with the most formative basis for making good student and classroom decisions. Using reflective problem solving to determine how and when to apply pedagogical principles will make you a professional teacher. A professional teacher is one who uses all the knowledge available to him or her to make the best possible decisions for students. List all the instructional methods you have learned from courses that you believe will make you an effective and professional teacher—for example, teaching science as inquiry or using a wide variety of authentic print sources to teach literacy. List all the theories of learning and motivation that you have learned from your courses: for example, Piaget's stages of cognitive development and Maslow's hierarchy of needs. List all the educational research you have learned that will guide you in making educational decisions: for instance, research on student motivation, effective classroom management techniques, and grouping strategies. Which of the educational theories that you have studied in this book and other sources do you feel will help you the most in the classroom? From an understanding of how students learn and what keeps them motivated, a good teacher will select the methods that best ensures learning. What is your current understanding of how to select the best instructional methods and activities to teach students? The types of instructional methods you select define you as a teacher. Your actions in the classroom and the decisions you make for your students are an important source of information about your philosophy of education. Listing the instructional methods you will use and, more importantly, why you selected them provides valuable insight into determining your educational philosophy. Determine your views on pedagogy by listing the components and describing how you will use these to be a reflective teacher.

A. List instructional methods you plan to use as a teacher.

B. List all the theories of learning and motivation that will inform your decision making.

C. List all the educational research you have studied that will guide your educational decision making.

D. Develop a narrative describing your pedagogy.

Step Four—Content Knowledge

Content knowledge is the academic knowledge and skills that you will teach. Your content knowledge will be acquired from your academic course work in general studies and your program majors, minors, or emphasis areas. A comprehensive understanding of your subject matter will provide you with the confidence as a teacher that you have knowledge worth sharing with students.

Review your course work and content knowledge that will make you competent in your field of study.

A. List all courses and experiences including majors, minors, and areas of emphasis that have developed your knowledge of content.

B. Develop a narrative describing what your content knowledge will bring to your teaching and students.

After considering the information and questions from these four steps, you should now be ready to write your educational philosophy. The information provided in your lists will determine the kind of teacher you will become. Write one or two paragraphs for each step. To help you brainstorm ideas, visualize yourself as a teacher in your own classroom. Imagine how you interact with students, what kinds of lessons you teach, and how your classroom is designed. These visualizations about your teaching are important windows of insight into what is important to you as a teacher. They are the best predictors of the kind of teacher you will become.

Once your paper is complete, share it with a peer you trust to make sure you are expressing your ideas clearly. Also, have someone check your paper for editing errors such as spelling, punctuation, grammar, and word usage.

REFERENCES

Bigge, M. L., & Shermis, S. S. (1999). *Learning theories for teachers.* New York: Longman.

Brooks, J. G., & Brooks, M. G. (1993). *In search of understanding: The case for constructivist classrooms.* Alexandria, VA: Association for Supervision and Curriculum Development.

Brophy, J. (1998). *Motivating students to learn.* Boston: McGraw-Hill.

Brophy, J., & Good, T. L. (1986). Teacher behavior and student achievement. In M. C. Wittrock (Ed.), *Handbook of research on teaching* (3rd ed., pp. 328–375). New York: Macmillan.

Darling-Hammond, L., Wise, A. E., & Klein, S. P. (1995). *A license to teach: Building a profession for 21st century schools.* Boulder, CO: Westview Press.

Deci, E. L., & Ryan, R. M. (1998). *Intrinsic motivation and self-determination in human behavior.* New York: Plenum.

Dulit, E. (1972). Adolescent thinking à la Piaget: The formal stage. *Journal of Youth and Adolescence, 1,* 281–301.

Eisner, E. W. (1985). *The educational imagination.* New York: Macmillan.

Friedman, M. I., & Fisher, S. P. (1998). *Handbook on effective instructional strategies: Evidence for decision-making.* Columbia, SC: The Institute for Evidence-Based Decision-Making in Education.

Fullan, M. (2003). *The moral imperative of school leadership.* Thousand Oaks, CA: Corwin.

Haberman, M. (1995). *Star teachers of children in poverty.* Indianapolis, IN: Kappa Delta Pi.

Kohn, A. (1993). *Punished by rewards: The trouble with gold stars, incentive plans, A's, praise, and other bribes.* Boston: Houghton Mifflin.

Leu, D., & Kinzer, C. (1995). *Effective reading instruction.* Englewood Cliffs, NJ: Merrill Prentice Hall.

Lortie, D. C. (1975). *School teacher: A sociological study.* Chicago: University of Chicago Press.

Marzano, R. J., Pickering, D. J., & Pollock, J. E. (2001). *Classroom instruction that works: Researched-based strategies for increasing student achievement.* Alexandria, VA: Association for Supervision and Curriculum Development.

Maslow, A. (1968). *Toward a psychology of being.* Princeton, NJ: D. Van Nostrand.

Piaget, J. (1966). *Psychology of teaching.* Totowa, NJ: Littlefield, Adams & Co.

Richardson, V. (1996). The role of attitudes and beliefs in learning to teach. In J. Sikula (Ed.), *Handbook of research on teacher education* (2nd ed., pp. 102–119). New York: Macmillan.

Shulman, L. S. (1986). Those who understand: Knowledge growth in teaching. *Educational Researcher, 15*(2), 4–14.

Weaver, C. (1990). *Understanding whole language.* Portsmouth, NH: Heinemann.

INTERNET RESOURCES

Kohn, Alfie

www.alfiekohn.org/

This is the author's Web site, with lists of his books and articles for further reading. Mr. Kohn questions the benefit of many common educational practices such as competition, rewards, gifted and talented programs, and standards-based instruction.

Learning Theory

www.funderstanding.com/about_learning.cfm

www.ucalgary.ca/~gnjantzi/learning_theories.htm

Two Web sites with a variety of general theories of learning.

Maslow, Abraham

www.ship.edu/~cgboeree/maslow.html

Similar to the Web site for Piaget, the Maslow Web site provides background information about the theorist and his theory of human motivation, the hierarchy of needs. The site provides an explanation of the hierarchy along with criticism of Maslow's ideas.

Motivation

http://honolulu.hawaii.edu/intranet/committees/FacDevCom/guidebk/teachtip/motivate.htm

Presents general principles of classroom motivation in a list format.

http://smhp.psych.ucla.edu/qf/motiv.htm

An extensive list of Internet sites that address student motivation.

Philosophy of Education

www.spaceandmotion.com/Philosophy-Education.htm

Snippets from a wide variety of philosophers (Plato to Haelhurst) are presented.

www.acs.ohio-state.edu/education/ftad/portfolio/philosophy/

This site offers an elaborate step-by-step process for developing your own philosophy of education, including an offer of feedback if you submit your writing to the site.

www.molloy.edu/academic/philosophy/sophia/TOPICS/phiedu/contents.htm

An online collection of the writings of great Western philosophers, including John Dewey.

http://atheism.about.com/library/FAQs/phil/blphil_ed_index.htm

A site of agnosticism/atheism describes how to develop a philosophy and provides resources to assist the process.

Self-Determination Theory

www.psych.rochester.edu/SDT/index.html

A Web site devoted to Self-Determination theory, a motivation theory developed by Edward Deci and Richard Ryan.

PART III

USING CASE STUDIES TO REFLECT UPON AND ANALYZE EDUCATIONAL ISSUES

FIVE

CASE STUDIES OF STUDENTS WITH EXCEPTIONAL NEEDS

The case studies in this chapter address the needs of students with the exceptionalities most often observed in classrooms. To prepare for the analysis of the cases, review your philosophy of education that you developed in the last chapter to connect your strategies for helping students to your belief system about teaching. Remember, the purpose of a philosophy of education is to actualize your beliefs as a teacher. If you fail to consider your philosophy before you begin, your problem solving may produce only superficial solutions to the problem. Teacher problem solving is superficial when it addresses only the obvious symptoms of the problem—noisy students, difficult students, low achieving students. To be reflective is to consider the larger instructional concerns—learning and motivation theory, developmental issues, and individual student history and needs—all necessary contributions to fully interpret the situation when attempting to solve the problem. Each case study poses questions but provides no definitive answers, because reflective problem solving and the teacher's own philosophy will determine how the problem is solved.

To help you identify the quality of your reflective problem solving, a rubric is included after each case study. The rubric does not provide best answers or solutions but comments on the quality of the problem-solving process itself. The levels of the rubric distinguish three levels of quality describing the problem-solving process. The first level describes a fully developed problem-solving process, where all available knowledge is used to solve the problem. This includes appropriate theory, research, instructional methods, and student data, as well as the values, opinions, and beliefs of those involved in the problem-solving process. The second level describes the use of partial evidence during the problem-solving process. For example, the reader's own beliefs and values can be included in the problem-solving process but not to the point of excluding more objective evidence. Objective evidence such as student scores, research, and theory provide a better basis for decision making than what is derived from a single individual's perspective. The third level represents the use of existing knowledge, preconceived ideas, stereotypes, and conventional wisdom that are not examined in relation to the evidence presented in the case study. The third level is not reflective. It uses common or popular wisdom that is of limited value because it does not take into account all knowledge about the problem that is available to the reader. It may also include preconceived ideas that the reader refuses to relinquish even when faced with evidence to the contrary. It produces overly simplistic solutions.

In addition to the reflective use of evidence to determine quality of problem solving, educational values are also included in the rubric. Values are included because they are impossible to eliminate from educational determinations. The rubric represents a specific value system about education. The value system is student centered, meaning that the educational needs of the student are considered first, paramount to those of the teacher, administration, or school bureaucracy. Often teachers and schools make educational decisions based not on what is in the best interest of the student but on what is easy and convenient for teachers and administrators or what supports the existing bureaucracy or culture of the school. Notice in the top level of the rubric that, when a conflict exists between various interests, it is the student's interests that are honored. A teacher who places the interests of the student ahead of self-interests is acting in a morally reflective manner.

In addition, recall from Chapter 2 our first analysis of case studies, the discoveries we made, and the lessons that were learned about reflective problem solving. Here is a summary of these:

- **Lesson One:** Never make rash judgments about students without checking the facts with reliable sources. Never label, belittle, or otherwise speak unkindly about students and their parents.
- **Lesson Two:** Use data about student achievement and behavior to make the best determination of how to help students who have problems.

- **Lesson Three:** Use educational theory to understand and make decisions about how to assist students and solve classroom problems.
- **Lesson Four:** Learn how to be reflective when solving problems and to recognize the importance of reflection in solving classroom problems and for your continued development as a teacher.

One of the most poignant moments in a teacher's career is when he or she realizes there are no simple procedures, four-step processes, or magic plans to solve tough educational problems. At that point, the teacher has to concede that good teaching means having good problem-solving skills. The teacher then begins to systematically apply his or her philosophy of education to the experiences of the classroom. Some of the case studies address controversial issues that are exceedingly difficult to resolve, but the discussion and consideration of different viewpoints will lead to a better understanding of the complexity of that issue. The vicarious experience of the case studies may even cause you to rethink and rewrite your philosophy.

CASE STUDY FIVE—ATTENTION DEFICIT/ HYPERACTIVE DISORDER: GABE SILVA (PART I)

Susan Sovinski's third year of teaching the second grade was, in her own view, going quite well. Her classroom was quiet, organized, and neat. Her classroom rules were posted for the students to see, and for the most part, they followed the rules. Everything was as smooth as could be expected, and Susan was proud of how far she had come since that first terrible year with undisciplined students and a confused, noisy classroom. During that first traumatic teaching year, many evenings found Susan numb with exhaustion, her ears ringing, and her head thumping. But in the years since, Susan had managed to improve her classroom management and organization skills and, most importantly, build rapport with her students so that learning was the primary classroom event occurring on most days. She was also relieved from the endless skirmishes of discipline and control that had dominated her first year of teaching. That is, until the middle of the year when a handsome bundle of energy named Gabriel Silva transferred into her classroom.

Susan objected to getting an additional student because she had as many students as the other second-grade teachers, and she viewed the social ecology of her classroom as in a delicate balance. Like the tropical rain forest where the elimination of one butterfly species could topple the entire forest ecology, she feared any additional alien element that might threaten her hard-won classroom serenity. And Gabe Silva was certainly a natural force to be reckoned with. He was attractive, almost beautiful, with thick dark hair and large brown eyes. He was outgoing, friendly, and talkative with all the students and seemed to thrive on creating an audience for his plans and monologues. When it was time for recess, Gabe would enter the playground like a cork popping from a champagne bottle. He would run across the playground at full throttle as if to throw off the sedentary dust of the classroom. He excelled at every game the second-grade boys played, including kickball, stickball, and soccer. He quickly took over the organization of the recess games, assigning teams and positions, arbitrating arguments over rules, and generally directing the other boys in their play. He was the first child on the playground each recess, and he was the last to leave the playground. He would remain on the field kicking the ball around until a teacher specifically called his name to come in. He would then dash across the playground and jump ahead of everyone else in line to be the first to enter the building. Susan watched him on the playground in amazement. She sighed. Where did all that energy come from? How could it be contained in her quiet, organized classroom?

Gabe was obviously of Latino descent, but his English was almost unaccented. His reading and math skills seemed nearly at grade level, but his grades were low because he failed to complete or turn in his work. He seemed interested in learning, but he was easily distracted. When Susan assigned work to be done at his seat, he started the page, but soon he was jumping up to sharpen his pencil, leaning over to talk with his neighbor, pulling toys from his desk to play with, or simply rummaging through his messy desk searching for things. When Susan stopped to check on him, he would look up from his desk, but often he had forgotten what he had been searching for. Susan thought his grades would improve if he were just more organized. He often seemed to complete his work, or at least part of it, but either he couldn't find it when it was due or he would forget to turn it in. After the students left for the day, Susan would go through his things and find dozens of partially completed assignments stuffed, wrinkled and torn, in his desk. Susan had never seen such as messy child. Gabe was a little better with the work he took home because he hadn't had time to finish it at school. He completed most of it, but, again, Susan would find the assignments in his desk long after they were due.

She asked the principal about Gabe's permanent records, but they had not yet arrived from his old school. During one particularly trying day, when Gabe talked with anyone close to him, Susan resorted to isolating him at the back of the room. Even from the back, Gabe would motion to students to join him at the back of the room where he would begin earnest and lengthy conversations. It seemed to Susan that the entire classroom was slowly, insidiously being infected with a Gabe virus that made them as noisy, active, and messy as he was. Susan conferenced with Gabe after class one day, and when she asked him if he understood the classroom rules, he said he did. She asked him why he didn't follow the rules—why was he always talking, getting out of his seat, and not completing his work? He hung his head and shrugged his shoulders; he didn't know why. He wanted to follow the rules. He liked school, he liked the other kids, and he liked her. He promised he would do better tomorrow. Susan didn't believe that for a minute, and she went to see her friend, the school's special education teacher. She asked the teacher to informally observe Gabe in her classroom the next time she had a few hours. Having briefly seen Gabe in motion on the playground, the special education teacher readily agreed. In the meantime, the special education teacher suggested that Susan collect informal achievement data on Gabe's basic reading, writing, and math skills.

The next day, Susan asked Gabe to find a book he liked and read it to her. He brought her one of the *Magic School Bus* books but didn't read a word of the text on the page. He made up his own narrative based on the illustrations, ignoring the text on the page. Susan gave him a second-grade primer with few words per page and simple illustrations. Gabe could read the primer and read particularly well when Susan covered the words and asked Gabe about the pictures and then covered the picture as he read the text. He was quite good at using context clues from the illustrations and was very imaginative in adding his own details and extensions to the story lines. Susan was convinced that, with the right books and support, Gabe could almost read at grade level. She then tried math, and Gabe balked at completing a full page of subtraction problems. When Susan used flash cards with a single problem and lots of praise for correct answers, she found that Gabe had memorized all the lower combinations and at least some of the higher ones. Writing was another matter. When she asked Gabe to write a short note home to tell his mother about a book fair to be held in the school, he started six notes on six pieces of paper and didn't complete any of them, leaving the pile of dirty, scribbled, torn papers under his desk. When Susan asked about his note for his mother, he said he had a good memory and he would tell her; he didn't need a note.

Based on the case study description so far, what do you think about Gabe and his behavior? Do you think Susan is overreacting, or is she prudent to take steps to seek help at this time? What evidence can you list that would indicate a need for intervention or a conference with parents? What do you think the special education teacher will report after her observation? What other action should Susan take?

When reviewing the evidence about Gabe, the information you learned from your special education or exceptional student courses would be helpful in contributing to the problem-solving process. Is Gabe behavior disordered (BD), learning disordered (LD), attention deficit/hyperactive (AD/HD), or just an energetic and spoiled child who needs clear boundaries and more discipline?

Your responses:

____

____

____

____

CASE STUDY FIVE—ATTENTION DEFICIT/ HYPERACTIVE DISORDER: GABE SILVA (PART II)

The special education teacher sat in the back of Susan's classroom and observed Gabe for two hours in the morning the first day and an hour in the afternoon the following day. She completed running records of all of his activities. She tallied the number of times he left his seat. She tallied the number of times he engaged other students in conversation. She used a stopwatch to time how long he focused on his assignments before he became distracted. She didn't stare at Gabe but looked at the entire class so that Gabe would not feel spied upon. During the observation, Gabe attempted to draw her into a conversation on his way to the pencil sharpener. He asked her who she was, what she was doing, and if she had an extra pencil. Based on what she had seen, the special education teacher suggested that they invite Gabe's parents to school for a conference, and she asked Susan to be prepared with his grades, samples of his assignments, and a short list of concerns to discuss with the Silvas.

The Silvas readily agreed to meet with Susan, the principal, and the special education teacher. Mr. Silva came in his work clothes and spoke good but accented English; Mrs. Silva was shy, spoke little, and didn't seem comfortable with her English. Mr. Silva said that Gabe was the oldest child in the family and that he had three brothers and sisters. He said that he and his wife were very interested in Gabe doing well in school and that the teacher should just tell him what Gabe needed to do. He would make sure Gabe did it, or he would be punished! Susan immediately felt uncomfortable. She didn't want Gabe to be spanked or punished. Gabe meant well; he wasn't mean—he was just driving her crazy. But she felt silly explaining that to these hardworking, earnest parents. To Susan's relief, the special education teacher jumped in to say that they were concerned about Gabe's grades; they thought he could do better if he were more organized, and she wondered if, with some practical steps, his grades wouldn't improve. She asked if Gabe brought home his assignments and did he have a regular place to complete them? Mr. Silva turned to his wife, and she spoke haltingly, saying that she asked about homework each day, and sometimes Gabe had it while other times he didn't. If he had homework, he completed it while sitting at the table as she was preparing dinner. Susan suggested an assignment notebook where she would make sure Gabe had his assignments each night and asked if Mrs. Silva would sign it and make sure he brought them back the next morning. Mrs. Silva happily agreed. Then Susan suggested that the kitchen was too noisy and distracting for Gabe's homework; maybe Gabe needed a quiet place in another part of the house to do his work. Mrs. Silva said that she had tried allowing him to work in his bedroom, but when she checked on him, he would have completed one homework problem and six other projects of his own device. To help him manage his work, Mrs. Silva had Gabe complete his homework in small parts. He would do a quarter of it, and then she would let him help her with dinner. She let Gabe tear up the lettuce or set the table. She felt he was more relaxed when he did a number of short activities instead of one long one.

The principal noted to Mr. Silva that Gabe was very good at sports, and Mr. Silva said that no matter how late he got home from work he always tried to play with Gabe in the yard. He kicked the soccer ball to him, pitched for batting practice, or he batted so that Gabe could shag flies. He said that Gabe always needed to keep busy and described how he was a great help with yard work or fixing the car or helping with the younger children. Mrs. Silva shyly related that her mother-in-law said Gabe was just like his dad and that as long as he was busy he stayed out of trouble. Mr. Silva told a story about Gabe when he was five and had been left alone in the garage. When they found him, he had dismantled the entire motor of the lawn mower. After that incident, Mr. Silva had bought Gabe his own broken lawn mower at a garage sale, and they often worked on them side by side.

Susan then suggested that, because Gabe was more inattentive and active than his peers, his parents should take him to a doctor to have him tested for AD/HD. Mr. Silva became visibly upset, and Mrs. Silva's eyes began to tear up. Mr. Silva said that he didn't want his boy on those drugs. The special education teacher said that identifying the condition didn't mean that Gabe would necessarily have to take drugs but that he would qualify for special services that could help him. She said that research had shown that most children did better with a combination of adaptive classroom strategies along with drugs to help distractibility and hyperactivity. Mr. Silva said that he didn't want his son in a special school or classroom. He would make him do better on his work. The special education teacher replied that if Gabe were identified as AD/HD he could still stay in Susan's classroom, and methods to help him learn would be designed just for him. She assured the Silvas that nothing would be done immediately; this diagnosis could not be made by the school but by a medical doctor. Also, nothing would be done without their signed agreement, and they would be invited to attend and participate in all planning meetings. The school would need their signed agreement to create and implement a classroom plan for Gabe before anything could be changed. Susan told the Silvas that although Gabe was nearly able to keep up with the other students now, in the future that could increasingly be a problem. The same could be true about his bossy behavior, which, by the fifth or sixth grade, could turn into aggression and fighting with other boys. The Silvas left the meeting looking worried but prepared to discuss and think about the next steps for Gabe.

Susan also left the meeting worried; she was concerned about Gabe and about herself. She wondered if she would be compelled to make numerous changes in her orderly classroom in order to accommodate Gabe. She didn't know how willing she was to change the methods that, before Gabe had arrived, had worked so well for her.

What do you think Susan will choose to do? Will she make her orderly classroom more accommodating for Gabe and the other students or will she insist that it remain the same? Should Susan willingly change or be compelled to make these changes? What are her rights as a teacher? What do you predict will happen to Gabe? Based on your philosophy of education and your values as a person and a teacher what would be your answer to the problem of Gabe?

Your responses:

____

____

____

____

Evidencing the use of the reflective problem-solving approach—by integrating your own philosophy and values and use of student evidence collected from classroom and school documents; observations; interviews by specialist teachers, parents, and medical professionals to produce the best educational decision for Gabe

(Continued)

(Continued)

Evidencing the emerging use of a reflective problem-solving approach—by using limited evidence to make the best possible educational decision for Gabe
Evidencing the need for a reflective problem-solving approach—by failing to make use of a systematic approach to problem solving and making educational decisions for Gabe based on what created the least amount of difficulty for Susan

CASE STUDY SIX—UNDERACHIEVEMENT: LASHANDRA JONES (PART I)

Lashandra was one of the most popular girls in the junior class. She was active in cheerleading, student government, the drama club, and a host of other social activities. Her SAT scores were in the top 5%, which did not surprise her teachers because she was a straight A student. In many respects, her teachers viewed her as the perfect student—she was well behaved, dependable, and highly motivated in her assignments, and she added a certain social sparkle to every class. At the same time, when Mr. Murphy, the high school counselor, examined Lashandra's perfect record, he discovered that Lashandra had academically "slacked" through her junior year. Her transcript revealed a series of courses that offered little academic challenge. Lashandra had been enrolled in the high-achievement track for English, but the English teacher was well known for giving every student in the class an A as long as the work was done neatly and reliably. Lashandra's record showed that she took only the required science courses. It also revealed that although she had enrolled in a calculus course the previous semester, she soon dropped it. When Mr. Murphy asked Lashandra about the course, she explained that after getting a B-minus on the first quiz she knew the teacher didn't like her, so she decided that she had better drop it because she didn't want to lower her GPA.

Mr. Murphy had seen students like Lashandra before; he knew the type. Students like Lashandra religiously follow the teacher's directions for every assignment. Such students are tuned in to their teachers and have an astonishing ability to predict what material will be stressed on tests. Lashandra overstudied for every test and repeatedly reviewed the text and memorized every possible fact that she might be asked to recall. She rarely read anything that was not required for a course. Working methodically within the guidelines and structure provided by her teachers, she had demonstrated no effort to be creative or to extend her talents in ways that were self-satisfying. Why would she? Her grades were excellent, her teachers loved her, and other students envied her. Most of her free time was spent pursuing an active and varied social life with many friends and boyfriends.

When Mr. Murphy discovered that Lashandra had ignored the schedule of courses he had suggested for acceptance at a selective university, he called her to his office. Lashandra informed him that she would be attending the local community college. Consequently, Mr. Murphy called Lashandra's parents to arrange a meeting to discuss Lashandra's final year in high school as well as her college and career plans. Her parents readily accepted the invitation. On the day of the meeting, Lashandra's parents arrived on time. To the counselor's momentary surprise, he discovered that Mr. Jones was black and Mrs. Jones was white. Mr. Jones was well dressed in a blue business suit and a conservative tie. Mrs. Jones was beautifully groomed with an expensive-looking suit and fashionably trendy shoes. Both parents were obviously proud of their daughter and her accomplishments and were happy to discuss her. Mr. Murphy began by asking if they were aware of Lashandra's plans to attend a community college rather than a more selective 4-year university. Mrs. Jones said she was aware of her daughter's decision, and she knew that it was based on Lashandra's wish to attend college with her boyfriend, who was not as academically gifted as Lashandra. Mrs. Jones expressed surprise at the counselor's concern, given Lashandra's 4.0 GPA and her level of involvement in extracurricular activities. Mrs. Jones stated that, although she was very busy running her own business, she was always happy to meet with her daughter's teachers and then went on to recount several of Lashandra's recent accomplishments, including performing the lead in the high school play and winning a local beauty contest.

Mr. Murphy responded that he was well aware of Lashandra's many talents and insisted that he didn't want her to waste them by attending an educational institution that couldn't possibly challenge her. Mrs. Jones countered by saying that while academics were important there were other qualities that were necessary for success in life. Becoming angry, Mr. Murphy said that he was surprised Lashandra's parents would allow such a talented girl to waste her time on beauty contests and community college boyfriends. Both Mr. and Mrs. Jones jumped to their feet. Mr. Jones shouted that Mr. Murphy had no right to speak to his wife that way and angrily demanded to see the principal.

Later, the principal reprimanded Mr. Murphy for his angry display with the Joneses, but they both shook their heads over the choices that Lashandra was making and what that said about their school and society in general.

What do you think about Mr. Murphy and his behavior with Lashandra's parents? Do you think he was justified in speaking his mind to her parents about Lashandra's activities? Was the principal justified in reprimanding him?

Your responses:

____

____

____

____

CASE STUDY SIX—UNDERACHIEVEMENT: LASHANDRA JONES (PART II)

You might be asking yourself if there is actually a problem to solve in this case study and how someone as successful as Lashandra could be considered a student with special needs. Lashandra is an academically gifted student who is working below her capabilities, and she is therefore an underachiever. If the goal of an excellent education system is to develop each student to the extent of his or her capabilities, then this one has failed Lashandra. Of course, Lashandra's parents and some of her teachers may dispute that conclusion.

The conflict between the counselor and the parents represents different value systems about what is important in education. When we talk about what motivates individuals to learn, there are two major perspectives—extrinsic motivation and intrinsic motivation. Proponents of extrinsic motivation operate from a behavioristic perspective and believe that the environment will provide all motivation for students to learn. They view the role of the teacher as providing a variety of extrinsic incentives such as praise, grades, prizes, and privileges to induce students to learn. Proponents of intrinsic motivation operate from a constructivist perspective and believe that motivation to learn is derived from within the learner and is based on internal interests and needs of the student. This second view assumes that in a supportive learning environment all students will want to learn, and they do not need external rewards to do so. In fact, they cite research evidence that demonstrates that the use of excessive rewards destroys a student's intrinsic motivation to learn. They have found that this is particularly true for topics that are of high interest to the learner and for tasks that require creativity and problem solving (Kohn, 1993).

Some teachers agree with this intrinsic motivation research and feel that rewards can diminish the student's natural love of learning and create students who won't attempt any learning task without the promise of a high grade, a privilege that means time off from school, a toy, food, or entertainment. Other teachers feel that much of school learning is boring to students and that many students wouldn't attempt to learn anything without the promise of a reward. They view rewards as an essential and useful classroom tool.

In Lashandra's case, Mr. Murphy represents the perspective of intrinsic motivation. Opposing his views, the Joneses represent the extrinsic perspective. You might wonder who taught the Joneses about behaviorism, but the truth is that both of these value systems are imbedded in our culture, and parents and teachers can ascribe to either. The debate over Lashandra's future is a clash over these views. Lashandra is an extreme case, as she seems exclusively motivated in her learning by extrinsic factors. Lashandra will only take courses when she is sure to get a high grade. She doesn't want to read or learn anything outside of school where no extrinsic rewards are offered. All of her attempts at "learning" revolve around what will please her teachers and earn her high marks, not what will excite her desire to learn or achieve for its own sake. You can imagine, and perhaps have even experienced, how seductive social approval and popularity are for a young woman in our society.

Mr. Murphy reacts to the clash of views with anger and by grieving over the loss of someone who is so capable of learning at high levels, but who will never attempt to learn anything based on her own preference. Lashandra's parents value her extrinsic accomplishments, so they cannot understand Mr. Murphy's perspective. They resent Mr. Murphy's concern as being disrespectful of what is important to them.

How can Lashandra's situation be resolved, or does it need to be? Do you believe that Mr. Murphy or anyone at the school can change what Lashandra values? Can they influence the choices she will make in her final year of high school and in her selection of a college? What would you say to Lashandra if she were your sister or friend?

This case study presents information about theories of extrinsic motivation and intrinsic motivation. Which of these do you value and want to promote in your future classroom? According to your philosophy of education, which theory better represents what is important to you?

Your responses:

____

____

____

____

Evidencing the use of a reflective problem-solving approach—if you used specific motivation theory to analyze the situation and to base your arguments about Lashandra's situation and future
Evidencing the emerging use of a reflective problem-solving approach—if you didn't use specific theory, but you discussed Lashandra's situation and used more general ideas and common knowledge about jobs she could obtain without a degree and the future quality of her life based mainly on your own experiences
Evidencing the need for a reflective problem-solving approach—if you determined that there wasn't a problem, and Mr. Murphy and others in the school should mind their own business. This view ignores multiple perspectives in education and the need to negotiate the case study controversy.

CASE STUDY SEVEN—BEHAVIOR DISORDER: WILLIAM "BILLY" STARK (PART I)

Everyone—all of the teachers and even the students at Southview Middle School—knew about Billy Stark. His reputation preceded him. He was the type of kid that everyone pointed out in whispers, and it was hard to miss him, even in a crowd. No matter what the weather, he always wore an oversized fatigue jacket, jeans, T-shirts, and heavy boots. His hair, if he didn't shave it, was dyed jet black and combed into spikes or gelled straight back. He was of average height, but he was so thin and scrawny that he appeared slight. Like a starved, stray dog, he loped and sidled around school—a clear misfit and outsider to observers. He didn't smell, but he appeared grungy and dirty. He smoked heavily and took drugs, often coming to school high or possibly pretending to be high. He was the kind of boy parents told their daughters to stay away from and teachers dreaded when they learned he was placed in their classrooms.

Sometimes such appearances in adolescents are misleading—the most ferocious-looking students will prove to be respectful and considerate. But not Billy Stark; in his case, his appearance was fair warning of what to expect from him. His reputation had preceded him from his last school, where he had been expelled. The teachers heard rumors, but they didn't know for certain if he had been expelled because he had brought drugs to school or because he had stolen fundraising money from the band booster's strongbox. None of the teachers wanted him in their class, and no one had any idea of how to handle him when he broke the school rules they expected him to break.

Mr. Salstic, the principal of Southview Middle School, was loved by the teaching staff. He was one of the few principals they had worked with who, rather than dealing with bus and cafeteria schedules during faculty meetings, actually dealt with student and instructional issues. The entire faculty met every other week, and the academic teams met for an hour once a week after school and daily for 20 minutes during their collaborative planning time. Mr. Salstic was committed to the idea that the only way to solve school problems was through teamwork and teacher input, and he worked hard to provide planning time for teachers so they could collaborate.

The principle of teamwork was evident when Mr. Salstic discussed where the new student Billy Stark would be placed and what kind of support services the teacher would need to help this challenging student. The seventh-grade teachers decided that Mr. Banta would be the best teacher for Billy, because of his low-keyed, nonconfrontational manner and his good rapport with students. The group also recognized that unless they were going to simply wait for

Billy to break the schools rules and then expel him as the last school had done, they would need support from many different sources. This would include the school counselor, who would meet with Billy regularly to track his adjustment to school; the special education teacher, because Billy was identified as BD, which made him eligible for special education services; and possibly tutors, because his records indicated that he was well below grade level in all academic areas. Mr. Salstic also wanted to keep in close contact with Billy's family and had already scheduled a meeting with Billy's father. The teachers left the meeting feeling better about the prospect of the new student, but they patted Mr. Banta on the back in sympathy for what they anticipated as a difficult assignment.

True to form, Billy was in trouble on the first day in his new school when he smacked another student on the arm with a book after he asked where he got his hair done. Mr. Banta didn't send Billy to the office because he wanted to deal with behavior problems within his own classroom, but he regretted not talking about Billy with the other students. Mr. Banta wasn't sure how to do this without invading Billy's privacy and labeling him as a troublemaker and a misfit. He needed the cooperation and understanding of all his students to see if Billy could make friends and fit in. Mr. Banta talked to Billy about the incident before he went to lunch. Billy denied hitting the student and then claimed that other people always picked on him, so he had to defend himself. Mr. Banta said they would talk to the school counselor after school. That same afternoon Billy was caught smoking in the bathroom by the janitor, which he also denied. Based on this, Mr. Salstic was glad the meeting with Billy's father was scheduled for the next morning.

Mr. Stark arrived on time the next morning. He had taken time off from his job as a pharmaceutical representative to meet with Mr. Salstic. He was honest with the principal about Billy's troubled school career. He described how at one point they had home schooled Billy because he was often in trouble for his behavior and had been making little progress in the regular school setting. Billy had also been in several special education programs and had been prescribed drugs to help him deal with his hyperactivity and aggression. Currently, Billy was particularly angry because his mother had suddenly abandoned the family. Mr. Stark admitted that in the past he had left all the parenting responsibility for Billy to his wife. He had worked long hours, and he had had a drinking problem that kept him away from home. But he was now sober, and he was prepared to help Billy and the school in any way he could. Mr. Salstic described the problems of Billy's first day and how the school planned to help and support Billy. He suggested that a united front would better convince Billy to change his problem behavior. Mr. Stark agreed.

Mr. Banta was an excellent teacher, but Billy tried his patience a dozen times a day. It was decided that, because he was so far behind, Billy would receive much of his instruction in the special education classroom, but he would remain for part of the day in the regular classroom with Mr. Banta. Here Billy could make friends and work to adjust to the routine of a regular classroom. During Mr. Banta's class, Billy was sullen, withdrawn, and sarcastic, and that was on a good day. On a bad day, he was angry, argumentative, and on rare occasions violent. During these violent incidents, Billy would suddenly erupt, throwing things across the room, shouting, and cursing. At these times, Mr. Banta would take the entire class to another classroom, leaving Billy alone in his rage. Mr. Banta would return when Billy had calmed down and talk with him, but Billy blamed others for his outbursts—the other students got on his nerves, his dad made him mad, his mother was a witch, Mr. Banta was unreasonable in his demands, and no one understood him. There were rare times when Mr. Banta could see glimpses of the kid Billy could be without the anger and the angst. He was intelligent, although not in conventional academics, but he had quirky interests and keen insight into the lives and motivations of others. He was good at historical and literary analysis, as long as he didn't have to read or write anything. He was uncanny in picking out the dysfunction of others, and he even had insight into roots of his own anger and antisocial behavior (his mother's disappointment with him), but that self-knowledge failed to translate into improved behavior. Mr. Banta recognized that working with Billy was taking a toll on him. He was emotionally exhausted and, as a result, didn't have the same energy and enthusiasm he usually had for teaching. The other students sensed this and were jealous. They told their parents, who called and complained about Billy's behavior and how the extra attention he received was at the expense of their children. Mr. Banta wondered what was fair and ethical in this situation.

In the special education resource room, where most of his instruction took place, the teacher found that Billy had so little confidence in his abilities that most of the time he refused to try the simplest tasks. It seemed that, while Billy had only the most basic of math skills, he could read on a third- or fourth-grade level. To gain insight into his learning, the special education teacher first conducted a functional behavior analysis and found that he needed to develop impulse control. She first attempted to use rewards such as privileges or tokens to modify his behavior, but Billy was so cynical and sarcastic or took advantage of such attempts, that she quickly abandoned the plan. For example, each time he was released from the classroom as a reward, he would be found in the bathroom smoking. He threw the tokens he was awarded across the room, and he complained about the lameness of the school's computer when he earned free computer time. The special education teacher tried to interest him in reading anything—including storybooks, comic books, and computer ads, but he usually refused. And if the teacher read to him, he seemed interested for just a short amount of time. He would then begin to make fun of the story, the characters, or even the teacher and how she pronounced certain words. Billy's comments could be biting, honing in on the insecurities, flaws, and weaknesses of others. The special education teacher remarked to Mr. Banta that for being nearly illiterate himself, Billy was certainly hypercritical about the efforts of others. The teacher thought that she could build from Billy's current interests, but the only interests that Billy would admit to having were video games, the more violent the better, and heavy metal rock music, the louder the better. Keying from that, the teacher found biographies of tragic rockers Kurt Cobain and Jim Morrison. She brooded about this activity, wondering if she were just providing a deviant's roadmap for Billy. Billy was interested for a short time in reading the biographies of the rockers and listening to their music, but, like everything else, he soon became impatient with the activity. It was as if something—emotional, social, or biochemical—always got in the way of his attempts to learn or change. The special education teacher wondered if an undiagnosed learning disability or neurological problem was being masked by Billy's home problems, school adjustment, and learning difficulties. At this point, it seemed too complex for even a team of health care experts to sort out, and she had Billy to deal with every day, whatever the root causes.

Soon after that, Mr. Salstic received a call from Billy's father. He thanked Mr. Salstic for everything that he had done for Billy, but he told the principal that he and Billy were moving to be near his family in Indiana who were willing to help him with the children. Learning this, the teachers were both relieved and disappointed. Months after he left, the teachers talked about Billy and the effort they had made on his behalf. They speculated that maybe they shouldn't have kept Billy; he was too extreme and perhaps he would have made more progress in a sheltered facility. Maybe more intensive therapy would have benefited him, but the school counselor said he refused to talk with her, saying he had been to plenty of counselors and all of them had been lame. Later, they heard that Billy had been placed in a juvenile detention center in Indiana, then they lost track of him.

What do you think of the effort Mr. Banta and the school made on Billy's behalf? Were these efforts too lenient, too tough, too uncoordinated? Would Billy have benefited from a "tough love" treatment? What assessment can you make about Billy's treatment and the ultimate outcome of his educational experience?

Your responses:

___

___

___

___

CASE STUDY SEVEN—BEHAVIOR DISORDER: WILLIAM "BILLY" STARK (PART II)

The case study of Billy provides a description of a student who had been diagnosed with a behavior disorder. Many of the characteristics described for Billy are typical, but Southview's response was not. Many schools and many teachers do not have the energy, resources, or compassion to truly attempt to help such difficult students. The conclusion of this case study was not satisfying, but it is accurate, because many such students are often passed from school to school until they drop out, or they are detained by another social service agency. Behavior disordered students can be difficult, time consuming, and baffling for parents, teachers, and other students. The confusion and helplessness that a new teacher might feel when working with a student with a disorder could be somewhat mitigated by an understanding of what creates the condition and how teachers attempt to deal with it. Courses about students with exceptionalities are very helpful in providing information and interventions in such a case; in addition, it is useful to review the theories discussed in previous chapters to see how they might apply in Billy Stark's case.

Maslow's hierarchy provides one explanation for Billy's disorder. If problems at home created an unstable and unhappy environment where he felt insecure and unloved, Billy might have arrived at school with little confidence in his ability to learn and to get along with others. If Billy's lack of confidence and difficulty with fitting into the school environment impeded his ability to learn skills and knowledge, his low achievement would have marked him as a school failure, further eroding his confidence and sapping his motivation to learn. Maslow's hierarchy describes a downward spiral of lack of success, leading to increased failure and decreased motivation. But while Maslow's hierarchy can explain in general terms what can go wrong in human development, it does not explain specifically what to do in such cases. The competing learning theories of behaviorism and constructivism attempt to do so.

The special education teacher first attempted to use behavioristic techniques with rewards and privileges to shape Billy's behavior to more positive outcomes. Behavior management technique has been the mainstay of special education and can demonstrate fast results. This was unsuccessful in Billy's case, and the special education teacher abandoned the plan. When behavior management is unsuccessful in demonstrating results, the behaviorist is quick to suggest that the reward the teacher offered must have been inappropriate for the learner. That which is rewarding is, after all, in the eye of the beholder. Determining acceptable rewards for rebellious adolescents can be particularly challenging for teachers. In Billy's case, his complete disdain for all rewards, except for those that contributed to his delinquency (like being allowed to leave the room and using that time to smoke), left the special education teacher with a dilemma best left to behavior theorists to solve.

The special education teacher then switched to constructivist methods. The reader should recall self-determination theory from Chapter 4. Self determination theory advocates the promotion of competence, relatedness, and autonomy as necessary for creating a successful learning environment. Billy's teachers attempted to engender his competence with instruction at a level where he could be successful, but Billy's skills were so low that, rather than facing the humiliation he felt with respect to his peers, he abandoned learning altogether. His teachers attempted to develop relatedness in the environment by placing Billy in a regular classroom for a portion of the day and by selecting a teacher, Mr. Banta, who related particularly well with students. Mr. Banta may or may not have been making progress with Billy—it was too soon to tell—but if he had reached Billy, then he could have provided a bridge to make connections with the other students in the class. For some students, all it takes is one strong connection to another human being who will provide positive support and mentoring, leading to new behavior. The proliferation of mentoring programs is based on this observation, but the connection has to be made by those two human beings, and it cannot be orchestrated by social welfare institutions such as schools and agencies.

The special education teacher attempted to provide autonomy, or choice, for Billy by selecting materials that were interesting to him, like the rock star autobiographies, but even this failed. Constructivist theories, such as self-determination theory, make assumptions about the relative health of the individual to pursue activities that lead to self-fulfillment and satisfaction in learning. With someone as cynical and self-destructive as Billy, all efforts on his behalf were twisted into a negative interpretation, which supported the negative reality Billy created for himself as he resisted a positive education outcome. Constructivist learning theory was actually correct in predicting Billy's responses, because the constructivist view holds that all experiences are filtered through the lens of the learner to be interpreted according to the learner's preconceived ideas or existing schema of understanding. To the despair of his teachers, constructivist theory predicted Billy's bleak outcome given his negative preconceived ideas and resistance to the interventions of the school. In this case, constructivist theory could explain, but couldn't overcome, the obstacles Billy faced in attempting to change.

The last consideration to make in an extreme case like Billy's is the use of community services to assist the school. Billy presented a number of self-destructive behaviors that made it difficult for the school to make a successful intervention, no matter how dedicated they were to helping him. For example, if Billy was using drugs regularly, this would typically act to mask the nature of the problem from the user's perspective, deluding him about the true nature of the problem. In other words, the use of drugs keeps the user in denial about the responsibility the user has to solve his or her own problem. With the approval of his father, substance abuse experts could have been called in to help Billy become sober. In a similar fashion, the severity of Billy's depression and anxiety might have required psychotropic drugs to level his feelings to the point where he could begin to form better relations with others and to support his attempts to learn the skills he would need to feel competent. Also, anger management might have been attempted in Billy's case. Billy's anger pushed people away from him and made it difficult for him to receive the help and support he needed as he attempted to build his skills. Last, his father might have benefited from social welfare services offered by the community, including family counseling, single parent counseling, and peer support. Overall, with extreme cases, the school and teacher need to be able to rely on and act in concert with all the services a community offers to support a family that needs assistance. A student's issues with learning are only one small part of the family equation, and it does no good for the school to work with the student if other negative forces are systematically impeding or destroying what the school is attempting to build.

The case study of Billy Stark provides an analysis of how educational theory can be used to attempt to solve a specific student problem. It also demonstrates that theories have limitations and that a theory cannot be applied and used to unfailingly solve a student problem. According to your philosophy of education, which view of motivation appeals to you when solving difficult student behavior problems?

Your responses:

____

____

____

____

Evidencing the use of a reflective problem-solving approach—if you were able to describe the benefits and liabilities of different theories from the narrative and how each could be applied to Billy's case to address his educational needs
Evidencing an emerging use of a reflective problem-solving approach—if you didn't use specific theory, but you discussed Billy's situation based on your values and experiences and how these applied to help a difficult student like Billy
Evidencing the need for a reflective problem-solving approach—if you determined that Billy should simply be incarcerated by educational or social services and be punished for his poor behavior. While this solution punishes Billy, it does nothing to address the educational problems of a troubled student

CASE STUDY EIGHT—ENGLISH AS A SECOND LANGUAGE: THE KITIPITIYANGKUL TWINS (PART I)

When Chris Kargas picked up her roster, she was surprised to find that she had twins in her first-grade class. Not only that, but the twin girls were from Thailand. Although it was common for big city districts to enroll large numbers of students speaking a variety of languages, it was a novelty for Chris's little community and small private school. The principal told Chris that he had met with Mr. Kitipitiyangkul, who had come to the United States to work in his brother's restaurant. The principal said that the father was excited about being in the United States and was happy to have his daughters enrolled in a private school. The principal said that the family spoke limited English but were learning fast. Chris asked the principal about support services for her new students, but he replied that she shouldn't worry because the twins were so young they would be fluent in English in no time. Chris wasn't so sure and wondered if she could find a Thai translator in their small town.

When Chris met with her class on the first day she could see that the twins were fraternal, not identical. Mary was tall and thin with serious looks and glasses. Susie was smaller with more babylike features. Chris wondered why the Kitipitiyangkuls had named their daughters such common American first names. Later she learned from the school counselor that the principal thought their first names of Pranee and Preeya where too hard to pronounce and remember, so he renamed them Mary and Susie. Chris was a little shocked—who did such things in this day and age? What was her school, Ellis Island? In any case, Mary and Susie it was, and Chris wondered what to expect. The girls were polite, quiet, and hardworking. They were self-sufficient and mainly kept to themselves. This worried Chris because she thought their language skills would benefit from more interaction with their peers. As the year progressed, the skills of the girls developed as divergently as their looks. Mary was the smart, serious one, while Susie lacked confidence and was slow to warm up to new ideas and activities. Mary could haltingly read the first-grade primer in accented English and was a whiz at addition and subtraction. Susie worked hard but struggled with every subject, and Chris couldn't determine if the problem was lack of confidence in English or another issue. Chris mulled it over and wondered that, if Susie's problem was limited English proficiency, why didn't Mary have the same problem? They were from the same home and the same age: Why didn't Susie learn at the same rate as Mary?

A few months into the fall semester, Chris was invited to dinner at the Kitipitiyangkul home. Suddenly Chris had firsthand experience of how teachers in other countries were honored and respected. Mrs. Kitipitiyangkul treated her like an honored guest as she and the girls served her an elaborate multicourse dinner. Mrs. Kitipitiyangkul explained that her husband was at work. He worked long hours, but he had prepared much of the food especially for Chris. Both girls were giddy with happiness to have their teacher in their home as they served her food. Here neither sister seemed shy or uncomfortable as they often appeared at school. Mrs. Kitipitiyangkul explained a little about Thai culture to Chris, who knew little. She was surprised to learn that the Kitipitiyangkuls were Buddhist; she had assumed they were Christian. Mrs. Kitipitiyangkul even presented Chris with gifts—a beautifully embroidered handkerchief and a little brightly colored paper fan. The gifts were exquisite, but they made Chris feel a little guilty. She didn't deserve the gifts, and she didn't deserve this honor. She really hadn't done very much to help the girls. They were just struggling along with the rest of her class doing the best they could.

Chris remembered the day she attempted to teach ordinal numbers in math by lining the children up and asking them to name their place in line such as "first," "second," and "third." Mary was fine, but Susie was increasingly bewildered and confused by the activity as Chris pushed her into different positions in the line and asked her to name her spot. Susie didn't know first from fifth. And Chris had no idea why. She thought about asking the special education teacher to evaluate Susie—perhaps Susie had a learning disability. But the school had so few resources that the special education teacher was already overloaded with students, and was it fair to label Susie as disabled when Chris really had no idea the nature of her learning problem? Maybe Susie just needed a few more months to learn English and then she would catch up to Mary and the rest of the class. Chris's guilt also led her to consider going to the fifth-grade teacher for information. His teaching always included multicultural topics, he had traveled a lot, and knew a great deal about other cultures—maybe he had some information about Thai culture and language that Chris could use in her instruction.

What do you see as the nature of the problem that Chris faces? Is she right to feel guilty? Is it fair that she receives little help from her school and yet is expected to teach students from a culture she doesn't know or understand? What steps do you think Chris should take?

Your responses:

____

____

____

____

CASE STUDY EIGHT—ENGLISH AS A SECOND LANGUAGE: THE KITIPITIYANGKUL TWINS (PART II)

How to educate children who speak a language other than English is one of the most controversial issues American schools face because it encompasses political and economic as well as educational issues. People hold sharply differing views about how recent immigrants should be taught English. It is a problem of increasing proportion, as it is estimated that there are as many as 8 million school-age children whose primary language is not English (Grossman, 1995). The American school system is struggling with how to adapt to the needs of so many children with so many different languages and cultures. So far it is uncertain which programs are best for children, and clearly Chris is caught in the middle of this American controversy; but schools struggle everywhere. Twenty states have enacted legislation or passed amendments establishing English as the "official" language of their state (Crawford, 1995, in Gargiulo, 2003), and five states prohibit bilingual education in their schools (Baca, 1998). California is one of the most diverse language states and, until recently, included school laws requiring bilingual education where children learned basic skills in their primary language. A referendum passed in 1998 called Proposition 227 mandated a maximum of 1 year of bilingual education for students with limited English proficiency before they were mainstreamed into English-only classrooms. The voter approval for this law surprised bilingual educators, with 61% in favor of the law, including 37% of Latino voters (Schnailberg, 1998). This legislation is particularly controversial when research suggests that fluency typically develops in children after approximately 2 years of instruction, and the deeper, more complex language structures necessary for academic success require an additional 5 to 7 years of instruction (Cummins, 1984, in Gargiulo, 2003). Some teachers fear that programs that transition students to English-only classrooms may be putting increasing numbers of children at risk for later school failure.

Ideally, every language-diverse student would be taught by a classroom teacher who is both bilingual and knowledgeable about the student's culture, but this is unrealistic. How many English-speaking people do you know who also speak Thai? Following are a number of approaches used to address the needs of bilingual students. You will see that some programs are more supportive of preserving and promoting children's bilingual language skills, whereas others are more interested in developing immigrants' English-language proficiency (Gargiulo, 2003).

Transitional Programs

Students are instructed in academic content areas via their primary language only until they are sufficiently competent in English, then they transition to all-English classes. The primary goal of this program type is to move students as quickly as possible to English-only classrooms. Most students exit after 2 to 3 years of instruction.

Maintenance (Developmental) Programs

These programs have a strong native language emphasis, where students maintain proficiency in their first language while receiving instruction in English. These programs promote a long-term approach with less emphasis on transitioning from the program and more emphasis on a solid academic foundation learned in the native language.

Immersion Programs

Immersion programs use English as the exclusive medium for instruction. Neither the student's primary language nor culture is incorporated into instruction. This provides a "sink or swim" approach to language development.

English as a Second Language (ESL) Programs

ESL is not a true form of bilingual education. Students typically receive instruction in English outside their regular classroom. There is an exclusive emphasis on English for teaching and learning; native language is not used in instruction. The program goal is to quickly develop English proficiency in bilingual students.

Sheltered English

Students receive instruction in academic subjects exclusively in English; no effort is made to maintain or develop proficiency in native language. English instruction is continually monitored and modified to ensure students' comprehension. The program goal is simultaneous exposure to the English language and subject matter.

The twins' case study is about applying educational programs to solve student problems. The type of program you would select and the educational and social goals you would want to achieve would speak to your values and what is important to you as a citizen and a teacher. Which of these language programs sounds the most similar to the program Chris was utilizing? What do you think would be fair education for the twins in terms of preparing them for life in the United States? What type of program do you think is in the best interest of our society? Which program would you select for Chris and the twins?

Your responses:

____

____

____

____

Evidencing the use of a reflective problem-solving approach—if you were able to describe the benefits and liabilities of the different language proficiency programs and how each might benefit the Kitipitiyangkul twins.
Evidencing an emerging use of a reflective problem-solving approach—if you didn't use the information about different language proficiency programs but were able to discuss how Chris could arrange her classroom to help the Kitipitiyangkul twins become more proficient in English.
Evidencing the need for a reflective problem-solving approach—if you determined that the Kitipitiyangkul twins should not receive special treatment to address their language difficulties. Instead, as recent immigrants, their parents should bear the responsibility for the twins' English-language acquisition. This represents a perspective where the student is viewed as the problem because they have needs that the educational system is unwilling or unable to address.

CASE STUDY NINE—RELUCTANT READER: AMY BRIGGS (PART I)

Each day during independent reading time Lee Shelby observed as Amy Briggs did everything but read. Each day during this 15-minute period students were allowed to select and read anything they preferred. Lee's classroom embodied the ideal of a print-rich environment with hundreds of books of all types and topics on shelves at the students' eye level. With everything from newspapers to recipe books to comics to joke books, students had a wide selection of reading material to choose from. With cozy spots like beanbag chairs, old easy chairs, and hammocks, students had many places to curl up in. With posters describing author studies and celebrities urging students to read, students had plenty of encouragement to sustain their efforts (Troyer & Paris, 1995; Turner, 1992). She even had a small geodesic tent donated from a sporting goods store, complete with flashlights, campstools, and fake campfire.

Lee consistently modeled a love of reading by talking about her favorite books and reading aloud each day to the class. The students always got to select the read-aloud book by classroom vote, and this time it was a Harry Potter book. To enhance the story-telling mood, students put on their Harry Potter glasses or black hats or capes or slung their legs over broomsticks. Lee's classroom instruction embodied a holistic approach to reading and writing. She encouraged students to write their own books, which were placed on special shelves in her library. Each day students journaled about their reading, and the class produced their own newsletter, which was sold to others in the school for a nickel to cover the cost of the printing. School news articles, photographs, drawings, cartoons, and a school advice column were written, edited, and laid out by the students. Computers were used to access the Internet for research, to e-mail pen pals, and to design and illustrate the newsletter and other classroom publications. Students even ordered new books from Amazon.com with the classroom book budget.

Lee often conducted workshops with other teachers describing her methods, and her principal was called on a regular basis to bring tours of teachers interested in seeing her classroom and to watch her model her classroom methods and activities. Each of Lee's classes usually included a few reluctant readers who with time and patience she was able to make modest headway in eliciting an appreciation for books. Books were, of course, the love of Lee's life. When other people were watching sitcoms or cop shows on television, Lee was curled up with a book in one of several favorite spots where she spent most evenings. She read everything—biographies, mysteries, science fiction, historical romance, and self-help books along with her professional journals and scholarly books. She had the complete collection of the Oprah Book Club selections. She subscribed to the *New York Times* Sunday edition so that she could read the book review section each week. She was dedicated to literacy and to bringing literacy to every child who was lucky enough to be placed in her classroom, and she was completely baffled by Amy Briggs.

Amy was alliterate; it wasn't that she couldn't read, it was that she didn't read. While other students were reading independently, Amy walked around the room pretending to select a book. Or she worked at the science or social studies center. Or she tried to sneak on to the computer, which she wasn't allowed to use during this time. Amy did anything but read. When Lee checked, Amy's skills in reading comprehension, vocabulary, and phonetic skills were completely on level for a 9-year-old. Amy balked when compelled by the teacher to read for an assignment, but after whining and complaining she would eventually complete her work. Amy was smart; she maintained above-average grades with little effort. She also demonstrated an amazing creativity to avoid all Lee's attempts to develop in her a devotion to literacy. Lee tried everything. She paired Amy with an excellent reader, hoping that peer mentoring would entice Amy to independent literacy. Amy allowed the other student to do all the reading while she daydreamed or attempted to distract the reader with other activities. Lee paired Amy with a struggling reader, hoping Amy would compassionately attempt to aid the reader in improving his skills. Instead, Amy enticed the naive student to engage in activities unrelated to reading such as talking, paper chewing, and spitting on the floor. Lee even resorted to bribing Amy by using the computerized reading series, *Ezcomp Reader,* a program that awarded points and prizes for each book read and test taken on the computer. Usually Lee only allowed the most underdeveloped readers to use the system. Lee felt that students should acquire a love for reading and an appreciation for seeking knowledge from books without extraneous rewards. Reading was reward enough in itself. But for Amy she allowed the reward of a pizza from the local delivery joint if she read a specified number of books. Amy scammed the system. She was an adept reader, so she quickly scanned the books she was reading (which were below her reading level), and then easily answered the simplistic recall questions on the computer test. She was ingenious at locating the thinnest, simplest, easiest books and reading until she had reached her quota and had her pizza, and then she stopped reading. Lee hesitated attempting using the computer program again—what would be her net gain, a fat Amy who still hated reading?

Not defeated yet in her struggle, Lee gathered material about Amy and her abilities—work sample, book reading lists, her achievement test scores, and her reading habits and prepared to put her case before Amy's parents at conference time. Amy's mother appeared for her appointment with Amy in tow. Lee brought forth the evidence and argued passionately about Amy's lack of interest in reading, but she couldn't convince Mrs. Briggs that a problem even existed. Mrs. Briggs just kept pointing to Amy's grades and completed assignments. She offered her own philosophy of child rearing that included the notion that too much was expected of kids these days. School was too stressful, and children should just relax and have fun when they got home. School learning was important, but so were other things—look at her, with just a high school education she had a great job at the local Zella window factory that paid great and had wonderful benefits. Amy was something of a tomboy like herself, and she liked playing sports and getting into things like the boys did in the neighborhood. Amy liked to work on cars and do yard work and work with her hands. She liked to stay active. Mrs. Briggs shared that she wasn't worried about Amy. Amy's grades were great, but her youngest, Kevin, was another story. The kindergarten teacher was already threatening to hold him back next year. But Amy, Amy was fine; Amy was her good girl and helper. Twenty minutes into the conference, Lee realized she wasn't going to get any help on the home front with Amy. Mrs. Briggs didn't particularly value reading herself, so how could she provide a role model of literacy for Amy? Wickedly, Lee thought there probably wasn't a single book, newspaper, magazine, or printed word in the Briggs household.

Going home and feeling defeated after the long grueling night of parent conferences, Lee considered her options and obligations to her students, particularly those like Amy. Who was Lee to say what was important in Amy's life? If Amy was destined to work at the Zella factory, then why did she need to read *Tuck Everlasting* or *Bridge to*

Terabithia? Who was she to impose her own values on a family who, by their own estimation, seemed to be living the American dream? Lee was so exhausted that night that she went to bed without reading.

What do you think Lee should do about Amy? Should she stop attempting to entice her to read? Should she continue to work with the family and Mrs. Briggs? What do you think Lee will do?

Your responses:

____

____

____

____

CASE STUDY NINE—RELUCTANT READER: AMY BRIGGS (PART II)

The next day Lee awoke to a whole new attitude and began to consider new strategies to motivate Amy to read. Lee had 12 years of experience as a third-grade teacher, and she wasn't prepared to throw in the towel on Miss Amy Briggs just yet! Lee thought about Amy's little brother and wondered if she sent home some simple story books and instructions and activities if Amy could be enticed to help him to learn to read. Her mother was right; Amy was a good kid. She would want to help her little brother learn to read, and in the process Amy might develop a sense of efficacy and appreciation for the power of reading.

Lee also considered this new information about Amy as a tomboy; it fit. If Amy were interested in building things and hands-on projects, the "How Things Work" series of books might be a way to intrigue Amy, particularly if Lee could organize a building project to parallel the book. If Amy were the tomboy that her mother claimed, then maybe she would be more comfortable working with a small group of boys on the project. Several of Lee's boys were marginal readers (who read far more than Amy), and they might also be interested in the building project. Lee thought she remembered that one of the books guided the reader through how to build a wooden slot car. Lee imagined that the Boy Scout leader would help the group and then they could hold a race and a classroom celebration. Math and measurement would be a great tie-in with reading, and Amy loved math.

A few weeks after the parent-teacher conference, Lee had begun organizing the slot car project and was excited about what might happen next. That day, during independent reading, Lee glanced up from her reading to mentally record what her students were doing and she couldn't find Amy. Lee silently got up and walked around the room glancing in corners, under tables, and into the tent. She found Amy in the corner curled in one of the beanbags reading *Julie of the Wolves*.

Lee Shelby's efforts might seem heroic on Amy's behalf, but the research evidence shows that teachers play a significant role in the achievement of their students. A teacher's sense of self-efficacy, that is, the teacher's beliefs in his or her skill and ability to teach, heavily influences not only how they view their students' ability to learn but also how they select classroom instruction (Bandura, 1997). Teachers with a high sense of efficacy operate with the belief that even difficult students are teachable through extra effort and appropriate techniques. They, like Lee Shelby, are experienced and committed to their students' literacy. Even when Lee felt defeated, she was able to rebound and plan her next attempt to help Amy. Self-efficacious teachers operate on the belief that, with extra effort and appropriate techniques, they can overcome negative family and community influences through effective teaching. In contrast, teachers who have a low sense of instructional efficacy believe there is little they can do if students are unmotivated and that the influence that teachers exert on students' intellectual development is severely limited by unsupportive or oppositional influences from the home and neighborhood environment (Bandura, 1997). Lee's success with her students resulted in a persistence, which was communicated to her students. Even if students had given up on themselves as learners, she had not. This teacher's confidence in the ability of students to learn, no matter the circumstances, communicated confidence to the students. Research shows that this influence is particularly powerful for young children, low-achieving students (Bandura, 1997),

> and minority students (Casteel, 1997). Low achieving students and students lacking confidence in their academic abilities are more vulnerable to the doubts of teachers with low self-efficacy and more influenced by teacher of high self-efficacy. High-achieving students overall are less influenced by their teacher's perceptions (Bandura, 1997). Knowing the extent to which a teacher's perceptions can influence student learning and motivation should caution new teachers to gain the skills they need to project confidence and competence to their students. Although this can be difficult for new teachers who are just developing a sense of themselves as teachers, the powerful influence they will have on their students should be an encouragement to attempt to be the best teachers possible.

This case study demonstrates that understanding theory can lead teachers to a better understanding of how their behavior can influence students in positive and negative ways. How does recognizing that your self-efficacy as a teacher can have an important positive or negative influence on student learning determine how you will prepare yourself for the classroom?

Your responses:

___

___

___

___

Evidencing the use of a reflective problem-solving approach—if you were able to discuss how theory describes and predicts the specific literacy methods that Lee selected to motivate her students to read and how Lee's high level of self-efficacy predicted the extent of her effort to help Amy become a self-motivated reader.
Evidencing an emerging use of a reflective problem-solving approach—if you were able to discuss Lee's instructional methods and their potential effectiveness with Amy but not how these are connected to literacy methods, learning theory, or teacher efficacy.

Evidencing the need for a reflective problem-solving approach—if you determined that Lee should not be overly concerned about Amy's reading habits, because if Amy's parents do not evidence concern about her education, why should the teacher? Some children are simply not intended to be readers. When this happens, it's not the teacher's fault. This represents the perspective that only those who share the values and culture of the school should be its beneficiaries. Those who do not share school values deserve their alienation from the benefits of education, and nothing should be done to alter this. Others would say the school should change in order to reach the student and family.

REFERENCES

Baca, L. (1998). Bilingual special education: A judicial perspective. In L. Baca & H. Cervantes (Eds.), *The bilingual special education interface* (3rd ed., pp. 76–97). Upper Saddle River, NJ: Prentice-Hall.

Bandura, A. (1997). *Self-efficacy: The exercise of control.* New York: Freeman.

Casteel, C. (1997). Attitudes of African American and Caucasian eighth grade students about praise, rewards, and punishments. *Elementary School Guidance and Counseling, 31,* 262–272.

Cummins, J. (1984). *Bilingualism and special education: Issues in assessment and pedagogy.* San Diego, CA: College-Hill Press.

Crawford, J. (1995). *Bilingual education: History, politics, theory, and practice.* Trenton, NJ: Crane Publishing.

Gargiulo, R. M. (2003). *Special education in contemporary society.* Belmont, CA: Wadsworth/Thomson Learning.

Grossman, H. (1995). *Special education in a diverse society.* Boston: Allyn and Bacon.

Kohn, A. (1993). *Punished by rewards: The trouble with gold stars, incentive plans, A's, praise, and other bribes.* Boston: Houghton Mifflin.

Schnailberg, L. (1998). Uncertainty follows vote on Prop. 227. *Education Week, 17*(39), 1–21.

Turner, G. (1992). Motivating the reluctant readers: What can educators do? *Reading Improvement, 29*(1), 50–55.

Turner, J., & Paris, S. G. (1995). How literacy tasks influence children's motivation for literacy. *The Reading Teacher, 48*(8), 662–673.

INTERNET RESOURCES

Attention Deficit/Hyperactivity Disorder (AD/HD)

www.ldonline.org/ld_indepth/add_adhd/add-adhd.html

The Web site LD Online provides information and answers questions about attention deficit/hyperactivity disorder.

www.help4adhd.org/en/about

The Web site of the national organization Children and Adults with Attention Deficit/Hyperactivity Disorder (CHAD).

www.nimh.nih.gov/publicat/adhd.cfm

A National Institute of Mental Health (NIMH) site that describes and defines AD/HD.

Bandura, Albert

www.emory.edu/EDUCATION/mfp/self-efficacy.html

A Web site devoted to Bandura's self-efficacy theory.

Behavior Disorders (BD)

www.state.ky.us/agencies/behave/homepage.html

The Kentucky Department of Education and the University of Kentucky host this Web site of information about childhood behavior disorders.

www.as.wvu.edu/~scidis/behavior.html

Web site includes an extensive list of strategies to help students with behavior disorders in a variety of classroom situations, including testing.

Bilingual Education

www.ncela.gwu.edu/links/biesl/

A Department of Education organization, the National Clearinghouse for English Language Acquisition (NCELA) Web site provides extensive links to information and resources for bilingual education.

www.multicultural-childrens-books-cds-friezes.com/bilingual-education.html

A publisher's clearinghouse of materials devoted to bilingual education.

www.ericfacility.net/databases/ERIC_Digests/ed403101.html

An ERIC Digest document that explains the research and the controversy over bilingual education.

www.rethinkingschools.org/archive/15_02/Edit152.shtml

This online newsletter reports information about bilingual education including issues and controversy.

http://ourworld.compuserve.com/homepages/JWCRAWFORD/biling.htm

This Web site provides insight into the controversy of bilingual education with discussion of various perspectives and issues.

Gifted and Talented Education

www.hoagiesgifted.org/
www.worldgifted.org/
www.gtworld.org/
www.nfgcc.org/
www.nagc.org/

These five national Web sites are devoted to the interests of gifted children and other individuals by providing information and support to teachers and families.

Parent Conferences

http://teachermentors.com/MCenter%20Site/ParentConfr.html

This Web site provides a list of tips to help teachers with what to do and say during parent conferences.

Special Education

www.cec.sped.org/

The Web site for the Council for Exceptional Children (CEC). This national organization is important for special education teachers and others who deal with children with special needs.

⁂ SIX ⁂

CASE STUDIES OF CURRICULUM, INSTRUCTION, AND ASSESSMENT

The following case studies deal with the "meat and potatoes" issues of lesson construction—curriculum, instruction, and assessment. Mastery of these topics is so essential for teachers that often entire education courses are devoted to them. Although each topic can be considered separately, they are also highly interdependent and related. Consequently, the type of curriculum a teacher selects determines the instructional methods he or she will use, and both of these determine the assessment methods that will be most effective to verify learning. For example, an inquiry approach to science requires instructional methods that are open-ended and hands-on with assessments that provide feedback on the quality of students' problem-solving skills. When instruction and assessment are mismatched, as with the teacher in Case Study Thirteen, students receive confusing messages about what the teacher believes is important for them to learn. When curriculum is mismatched with the needs of students, this also hinders the learning process. This situation occurs in Case Study Ten, in which an inexperienced teacher selects a lesson without consideration of student needs. Case Study Twelve also presents a problem of mismatch, in this case, between the instructional methods used by the teacher and the needs of a particular student with a special talent.

The case studies in this chapter emphasize assessment, because in the current political climate, school assessment is a high-profile issue. Many citizens, parents, policymakers, and politicians believe that extensive testing with predetermined standards and holding teachers and students accountable will produce higher levels of learning. Sometimes this is termed "high-stakes assessment." In high stakes systems, schools that fail to improve their test scores can, for example, be closed or have their administration taken over by outside groups, such as departments of education or for-profit corporations. Although it is debatable if high-stakes assessment truly improves student learning (Bracey, 2003), for the foreseeable future, it will be a part of every teacher's life. For this reason, teachers need to find ways to reconcile their own philosophy and values about education with the policies and mandates that are decided for them by others. Case Study Eleven explores this difficult problem with an idealistic biology teacher.

As you review the case studies, you should remember to be reflective in your problem solving. Reflection, according to Dewey, operates at three levels (Rodgers, 2002). The first level is reflection about specific classroom decisions. This includes planning lessons, lesson implementation, and the steps taken after instruction to determine what comes next for students. At each point during the lesson, the reflective teacher decides the best educational solutions for students. This level of reflection is the one most typically described by teachers. The second level of Dewey's reflection describes what teachers should think about when they reflect. Dewey thought teachers should consider theory and research as they attempt to solve classroom problems. Recall that theory and research were described in Chapter 4 as part of the content of reflection. The use of theory and research in problem solving expands the teacher's perspective beyond a single person's experiences to include the collective experiences of the many educators who developed the theory and research. As you reflect, you should consider the content of your child development, educational psychology, and methods courses as examples of this type of knowledge to use in classroom problem solving. Dewey's final level of reflection includes consideration of what the teacher hopes to accomplish with education, that is, the kind of learner, citizen, and society the teacher hopes to create through his or her teaching. Dewey wanted education to create democratic citizens to participate in a democratic society. The reader may have other educational goals such as creating an environmentally aware citizenry, a literate citizenry, or citizens committed to creating a just and equitable society. You should consider that if you were to run into a former student years later at the mall, what kind of person would you want to encounter? Answering that question will provide insight for what is important to you.

CASE STUDY TEN—INATTENTIVE CHILDREN: STUDENT TEACHER (PART I)

Jana is an elementary education major and participating in her first field experience in a first-grade classroom. Jana had recently observed the class and conferenced with the classroom teacher about developing and teaching a lesson to fulfill the requirements of her reading methods course. On the day of the field experience, she arrived prepared to teach a lesson on story sequencing, using the book *The Little Red Hen*. She made props that she brought to help the students act out the sequence of the story. Jana knew that her university instructor would observe her and provide feedback to help her improve her teaching. Jana was nervous about her lesson but excited about finally teaching "real" children.

Jana arranged the group of nine first graders on the floor in a corner of the classroom and began her lesson by announcing that she would read them a story about a hen. After she finished the story, she handed out the props and asked students to retell the sequence of the story as they held up their props. She was 10 minutes into a 20-minute lesson when, to her surprise, the students started acting silly and disinterested in the lesson. They didn't seem to remember the sequence of the story and with nothing else to do they waved the props around, rolled around on the floor, talked with each other, and were generally inattentive to Jana's request to settle down. Jana didn't know what to do. She felt increasingly flustered as the students got noisier and more active. She looked around to spot the teacher and wondered why she didn't do something to make the students behave. Finally the lesson time was up, and Jana and the university instructor talked about what had happened.

When the instructor asked her about the lesson, Jana expressed disappointment with the children, "I don't understand why the kids were talking and playing when I was trying to teach. I spent four hours last night cutting out and coloring the props. They were so cute." The university instructor asked Jana what she had done at the beginning of the lesson to prepare students to learn. Jana slowly shook her head and replied, "I didn't think about it. It was such a cute lesson, I just knew the kids would love it."

Given this description of events during the case study and Jana's lesson, what do you think created the problem? Are the students to blame, as Jana suggested, by not appreciating her effort in creating an interesting lesson? Are the lesson activities the problem? Or does the problem lie with Jana's lesson implementation?

Your responses:

____

____

____

____

CASE STUDY TEN—INATTENTIVE CHILDREN: STUDENT TEACHER (PART II)

The instructor responded to Jana by stating, "It is the responsibility of the teacher to use techniques to engage and motivate students to learn. Now, what could you have done at the beginning of the lesson to make sure the children were ready to learn?" Jana shook her head; she was so rattled by the experience that she didn't know what to say. The instructor asked, "Could you have explained to the students about what they were about to learn? Could you have provided clear directions about what they should listen for as you read the story?" She went on, "How did you expect the students to know that you wanted them to remember the sequence of the story if you didn't tell them that ahead of time? No wonder they were confused! At least, Jana, you could have made an assertive effort to gain their attention before you began the lesson by making eye contact with each student. Jana, I'm surprised that you made one of the most common 'new teacher' mistakes. You started the lesson without making sure the students were attending." The instructor then asked, "Why did you pick that particular lesson?" Jana told her that the book had been a favorite of hers as a child, and she had been enchanted by a lesson plan and a pattern for the props she found in a teacher magazine. Jana assumed the students would love the lesson because she had. The instructor noted, "So, you were thinking of yourself and what you like and not what the students wanted or needed." That immediately upset Jana and her eyes started tearing up. "No, it wasn't like that. I don't want to be a selfish teacher, I want to be the teacher who the students love and who they learn a lot from." "Well then," said the instructor, "What have you learned during the last four weeks in class about how to develop lessons for children?" Jana was a good student; she knew the answers. Teachers should consider the prior knowledge of students, their developmental levels, the content or standards of the curriculum, and the students' interests. Jana's instructor told her to ask the teacher about these elements when she went back to the classroom. Then the instructor asked what the teacher had told her about the students prior to the lesson. Jana said the teacher had told her she could teach anything she wanted. When Jana told the teacher that she had already picked a great lesson the teacher didn't question her further. The instructor said, "Jana you are going to be a great teacher someday, but you have to do some work to get yourself there. Plan your lesson with the students in mind next time and see how the lesson goes."

What do you think about the feedback Jana received about her lesson? Was it fair? Do you think the university instructor was harsh with Jana? What information do you think teachers should use when they plan lessons? What do you predict Jana will do for her next lesson?

Your responses:

____

____

____

____

Evidencing the use of a reflective problem-solving approach—if you were able to discuss how Jana's lesson planning should have included specific use of student information such as prior knowledge, developmental levels, and specific interests in order to match instruction to student's needs
Evidencing an emerging use of a reflective problem-solving approach—if you were able to discuss why Jana's lesson plan failed in practical terms but didn't

(Continued)

(Continued)

connect her instructional problems to learning theory, developmental levels, or the specific needs of the students
Evidencing the need for a reflective problem-solving approach—if you determined that the university instructor was unfair to Jana. If Jana had worked hard to plan and develop the lesson then it was not her fault that the students were not interested in the lesson and didn't learn. This view blames the children for the failed lesson rather than placing the responsibility with Jana and how she planned.

CASE STUDY ELEVEN—HIGH-STAKES ASSESSMENT: BIOLOGY TEACHER (PART I)

At 22 years old, Ellie Leclere had just landed her first position as a biology teacher in a large rural high school. Ellie was beside herself with excitement about her new classroom and students. She worked all summer to plan activities aligned with the state's core content for science and to write a state grant that would fund her students' participation in a clean water project. The teacher education program from which she had graduated emphasized the inquiry approach to science, and Ellie was ready to bring that approach to her high school students.

During her own high school years, Ellie had been an excellent student in all subjects, including the sciences, but she was often bored by the endless regurgitation of content from textbooks to tests. It wasn't until she took a biology course in college that she even considered science as a major. At her college, they taught biology as an inquiry approach. This approach allowed students to investigate real problems in biology rather than just memorize information. As part of her course work, Ellie conducted investigations of the quality of the water and soil in the local wetlands, and she helped to count the number of a particular type of rare hummingbird. The professor leading the program, Dr. vanAutry, was such an inspiration to Ellie that she selected biology as her major and asked Dr. vanAutry to be her advisor. Ellie found Dr. vanAutry to be a challenging teacher who exposed her to the most compelling ideas.

Now, after completing all her course work in her major, her professional education courses, and finally her student-teaching semester, she was ready to bring that excitement to her own students and teach in the same manner that had inspired her to love science. The clean water program that Ellie used to organize her curriculum trained high school students in the collection of water specimens and the detection of specific chemical and biological contaminates. The project was designed to be an environmental watchdog for industrial and farming corporations as it trained students to protect and appreciate the environment. The area where Ellie lived was a naturalist's paradise, with several large public lakes, wetlands preserves, and wildlife sanctuaries. Ellie wanted her students to appreciate where they lived and protect it when they graduated and became adult citizens. She also wanted to bring the science from textbooks to life with a project that would make a real difference in their community. The students would collect water samples from their area that would be sent to the state's environmental testing facilities, where they would be analyzed and recorded. If harmful levels of contaminates were found, the offenders would be notified, as would the students.

The school hired Ellie based on her high grades and her excellent references. During her first days at the school, she excitedly explained her plans and projects to her new colleagues. They seemed cool to her ideas, but she dismissed this. It didn't matter what the other teachers were doing; Ellie was certain hers was the best approach to teaching science. The obstacles to her plans began with the other science teachers, but they escalated as the year progressed.

The teacher assigned to Ellie as her mentor wanted to know why she wasn't using the science textbook. He explained that the textbooks were new and the textbook committee had been careful to select a series that would support the core content for the state achievement test. He wanted to know, if Ellie didn't use the textbook, how would she know she was teaching all the concepts that were required for the test? Ellie assured her mentor that she had completed a curriculum alignment the past summer and that she had worked most of the concepts into her activities, projects, and lectures. She found that time was her worst enemy, as it was impossible to thoroughly teach all the concepts. Ellie also explained that she didn't think the textbook was very useful. What was the point of assigning textbook chapters when she knew the students wouldn't read them? Besides, she had better ways to teach. The mentor suggested that Ellie should assign the readings during class time when she could monitor the students' reading and then immediately test them. The students wouldn't have an excuse not to complete the assignment. Offended by this suggestion, Ellie angrily fired back, "Except for the students who can read and couldn't care less about science!" Looking tight-lipped and frustrated, Ellie's mentor told her to use the textbook. Equally frustrated, Ellie ignored the command and proceeded with her plans.

Several weeks later, the department chair stopped by her room after school to ask how things were going and to out find if she needed anything. Ellie was tempted to tell her about her mentor's stupid suggestions but held her tongue (she didn't want to be known as a troublemaker). The department chair held up the test scores of her students from the previous year and asked if Ellie had seen them. Ellie replied that she had. The department chair informed her that the scores were some of the lowest in the district and reminded Ellie that she had been hired to help increase the scores. The chair asked what plans Ellie had made to improve the test scores. Ellie replied that she had been hired to teach science, not teach the test. Besides, with the instruction she was using, she was certain they would see improved test results and learning from experiences that would last the students' entire lifetime. She explained that she wanted to produce citizens who were environmentally aware and locally active. Their community had a great deal at stake. Several new agri-corporations had been developed, and there had already been questions in the newspaper about the impact these were having on the local water table. The department chair snapped that Ellie should have a little more concern for things closer to home. If the science scores didn't improve in the next few years, the school would be declared in crisis by the state, and she and the rest of the science teachers might be looking for new jobs!

This time Ellie was shaken. She went home in tears, and as she thought over the conversation, she tried to conceive of a way she could work on both her project and still drill students on core content. The students had been working in small groups, conducting investigations of environmental conditions in the area so they would know what to anticipate when they began collecting samples in the field. She allowed the work of the investigations to continue for three days a week, but for the other two days she lectured and administered pop quizzes. The effect of this change on her students was immediate and obvious. On lecture days, students who normally came to class early to spend time on the computer and students who asked Ellie dozens of questions slumped in their seats and didn't bother to pretend they were paying attention to her lecture. She didn't blame them. They felt betrayed by her promises of what to expect in her classroom and they were right that she had betrayed them. She was considering cutting the lectures to only one day a week when her principal asked to meet with her after school.

That afternoon he told Ellie that he had been reviewing transportation requests and had noticed that she had planned several extensive field trips for her students. He wanted to know the purpose of the field trips. Ellie explained about the project and the grant. She assured the principal that after the students were trained during one Friday and weekend, she would only need afternoon field trips to travel to sites to collect samples. The principal wanted to know how Ellie justified the students missing their other classes. Had she obtained permission from their parents? He also wasn't sure it was good idea to take students on trips into the wilderness. A few years ago a student had set a field on fire while on a field trip. You never knew what students would pull. And who would pay for the buses and meals for the trips? Ellie said the grant would pay the school for the buses but she hadn't thought about food. Maybe the cafeteria could pack lunches. She hadn't thought to budget for food, and the grant funding was tight. The principal wanted to know if she had checked with the athletic director about the bus schedule. He was certain he had seen conflicts on some of the dates. If the team needed the buses to travel to games, they got first priority. The athletic schedule had been planned for months.

The principal shook his head and told Ellie that she needed to go back and do some more thinking about her project. He told her that she needed to realize that it was a big school and she couldn't go off and do her own thing without thinking about how it would affect others. He was freezing her grant budget until he had more details, in *writing,* about her plans.

Ellie felt sick with disappointment. Now it seemed that everything—her project, her way of teaching, the way she was going to make a difference in the lives of her students—was in jeopardy. They were all against her, and she couldn't understand how they were allowed to do this. Could they force her to teach in a boring traditional way that she knew was wrong and would simply create another generation of kids who hated science and who would never understand its importance in their lives? This was not what she had expected. This was not why she had become a teacher.

In an effort to save her plans and her self-esteem, Ellie met with one of her friends from college who was also in her first year of teaching. Ellie poured out her story along with her frustration and disappointment. To her surprise her friend was not supportive. She admonished her, "Oh, Ellie, you are so naive and idealistic. You are in a real school now and you have to get with the program. You can't do everything vanAutry taught you; she hasn't been in a *real* high school in *thirty* years!"

What do you think Ellie should do? Should she continue with her project in spite of opposition? Do you agree that she is naive? Should she teach in the traditional manner until she has worked out the logistics of her project? Should she quit her job? Do you think she will ever be able to teach in the way she feels is most beneficial at that particular school?

Your responses:

____

____

____

____

CASE STUDY ELEVEN—HIGH-STAKES ASSESSMENT: BIOLOGY TEACHER (PART II)

> Feeling defeated, depressed, and under extreme pressure, Ellie conducted the rest of the school year in the traditional lecture manner as her colleagues and supervisors expected. Later, she learned from one of her friends at the Environmental Action League that one of the new agribusinesses in her area, an enormous hog farm, had been cited for contaminating the ground water in her region with fecal waste product. The developer was one of the town's most prominent citizens, and it was likely there would be lawsuits on both sides with a lot of messy press coverage. Ellie was stunned. Was it possible that her administrator had stopped her classroom project for fear of embarrassing an important member of the community? She would never know because she refused her teaching contract for the following year and applied to a school of chiropractic medicine.

How do you view Ellie's decision to leave teaching? Does this seem like a rational response when Ellie could look for another school that is a better match to the way she wants to teach? Who should bear the responsibility for the loss of a talented young teacher? Ellie, who was not suited to the constraints and demands of the school, or the school that would not accommodate Ellie's teaching requirements? Who was the biggest loser?

Your responses:

____

____

____

____

Evidencing the use of a reflective problem-solving approach—if you were able to discuss the complexity of the issues facing Ellie. The controversy examines the rights of professionals like teachers to govern their classroom decision making versus the rights of the community to demand the education they feel is most appropriate for their children (including high scores on standardized tests).
Evidencing an emerging use of a reflective problem-solving approach—if you were able to articulate one side of the debate of teacher rights versus community rights, but not both. In educational issues where opposing rights are in conflict, it

(Continued)

(Continued)

is important to see both sides of the issue to understand the nature of the debate and to seek compromise when designing solutions.
Evidencing the need for a reflective problem-solving approach—if you determined that Ellie should quit teaching because she isn't allowed to teach the way she would like, or if you determined that she should capitulate and do as her administrators told her. Both responses take an extreme position on the issue that ignores the complexity of the situation and the possibility of developing a compromise solution.

CASE STUDY TWELVE—INAPPROPRIATE SCAFFOLDING: CASSIE BRIGHT (PART I)

For the first time in her all her years of schooling, sixth grader Cassie Bright dreaded when it was time for writing. Cassie sat in her seat secretly working on a poem about a lark with clipped wings scrabbling around in the bottom of a cage, imagining a meadow full of light and breeze where birds would blithely soar. When Miss Neussbaumn announced writing workshop time, Cassie resentfully hid her poem from her teacher and slowly pulled her writing journal from her desk. She unhurriedly got out her pen and resigned herself to frustration. Miss Neussbaumn stood at the front of the class and gave instructions about how the students would spend their time that day. Today it would be peer editing, and thank goodness, thought Cassie, she was paired with Will, whom she had known since first grade. Working with Will on his paper, Cassie knew that she could help him. Will wrote just as he acted—he was full of energy, ideas, and fun, but he never finished anything he started and his sentences seldom completed a thought. Will's stories were riddled with sentence fragments and evidenced a complete lack of concern for proper punctuation. He and Cassie would spend a satisfying 20 minutes revising sentence structure to complete his thoughts, agreeing upon punctuation and narrowing his thesis to a few developed ideas. She would enjoy helping Will, he would be grateful, and Cassie would be spared another session with one of the girls in class. These more advanced writers would frustrate Cassie with silly, simple, illogical corrections to her work. After she and Will worked together on his paper, Cassie would read hers to Will.

He would tell her that it was great or admit that he didn't understand it or ask her to write about an interesting topic (like dinosaurs, his favorite), but at least he would be honest. She could trust his interpretations of her writing because they were based on his own sweet, honest self. With many of the girls, Cassie never knew what to expect, and she distrusted their motives, which seemed based on jealousy, peer competition, and spite, evidenced in the manner in which they marked up and corrected her papers. They had to find something wrong with her writing, Miss Neussbaumn told them so. When they didn't understand her writing, rather than admit this, they punished Cassie by maliciously changing her writing. To Cassie, the entire process was an insult to her intelligence, for Cassie was without question a gifted writer.

Miss Neussbaumn's class should have been a safe haven for Cassie, which is what she and her mother had expected. Miss Neussbaumn was newly trained in the writing workshop method of instruction. In their very traditional school, Miss Neussbaumn was the only teacher with such training. At the beginning of the school year, Miss Neussbaumn had spent considerable time explaining to Cassie's mother how excited she was and how she couldn't wait for the new school year to begin to implement the new methods. Miss Neussbaumn confessed that in the past she had disliked writing and had avoided teaching it. Her writing instruction had been traditional, and she recognized how this caused her students to hate and avoid writing. But she would change all that now that she had a precise plan for how writing instruction would take place in her classroom every day for the entire year. She would include writing and reading workshop each day in her class, where students were free to write on their own topics and make their own reading selections.

Miss Neussbaumn would include all four stages of the writing process (Solley, 2000; Yopp & Yopp, 2001). She included prewriting because she had learned that writing experts claimed that as much as 80% of writing time should be spent on prewriting activities. Miss Neussbaumn would require three prewriting activities for each assignment. Students would write in a journal each day to record their free-flowing writing ideas, then students would draw a picture of their proposed writing project, and finally they would create a web to brainstorm ideas for the paper. This would ensure that students had something interesting to write about. Nothing was worse for novice writers than staring at a blank sheet of paper.

Next, students would thoroughly develop and edit their work by completing four drafts of their projects. Students would proof their writing using an editing chart that Miss Neussbaumn had already developed for them. The chart included questions about the introduction, capital letters, paragraph structure, spelling, punctuation, grammar, and the ending or conclusion.

Last, students would celebrate and publish their writing by laminating the pages and binding them into books. The principal had already agreed to place the school's laminating machine in Miss Neussbaumn's classroom. Using the four stages of the writing process, Miss Neussbaumn would no longer avoid the topic that had made her feel uncomfortable; she was ready to embrace writing instruction with all of her enthusiasm. Each day of the week, during writing workshop time, Miss Neussbaumn assigned a specific activity that the students would complete without fail. All of this structure was designed to scaffold student writing, that is, provide the activities and teacher and peer assistance to promote high levels of learning (Dixon-Krauss, 1996).

Miss Neussbaumn's plan had been wonderful news to Mrs. Bright, because Cassie had been reading and writing from the time she was 4 years old, but her teachers often didn't know how to deal with Cassie's talent. For the most part, they simply ignored it and let her read and write as she pleased. Cassie always earned excellent grades in those subjects but received little feedback or teacher support for her work. Mrs. Bright sometimes felt guilty about Cassie because she had not been able to send her to special workshops or camps to nurture her talent. Happily, Mrs. Bright was a voracious reader, so there were always books around the house for Cassie to read. But now with Miss Neussbaumn, Cassie would finally have a teacher to understand and nurture her talent and skills.

For Cassie, sheer disappointment was part of her frustration. Like her mother, Cassie had held high hopes for Miss Neussbaumn as a writing mentor. These hopes had turned into a nightmare of boring prewriting assignments, endless unnecessary drafts, trivial feedback on her writing, and painful peer editing sessions. Her initial hopes had lead Cassie to bring Miss Neussbaumn a portfolio of her writing projects. These projects extended from when she had written plays with dialogue for her dolls and stuffed animals before she began kindergarten to the past year when Cassie had written a collection of short stories about animals and a book of poems about life in school. Miss Neussbaumn glanced at Cassie's writing, smiled at her, and said, "We are going to have such fun this year! Everything is already planned and you are going to love it, Cassie!" To Cassie's utter shock and horror, she realized that Miss Neussbaumn didn't see her and her special talent at all. Miss Neussbaumn treated Cassie like every other student in the class. She expected her to complete the same activities, in the same order, in spite of the obvious evidence that Cassie didn't need those activities. Still, Cassie needed something from Miss Neussbaumn that was quite different from the needs of the rest of the students in the class.

To Miss Neussbaumn's credit, the other students, including Will, genuinely benefited from her new instruction, because so much of their writing instruction had been of the traditional grammar, handwriting, and spelling variety. These activities, along with a few story starters or writing prompts, constituted Miss Neussbaumn's entire writing instruction. Some writing researchers call this type of writing instruction "ghetto instruction" because it deprives students of the support they need to become independent writers. Now, Miss Neussbaumn allowed some degree of choice for students in selecting their topics, and Miss Neussbaumn's activities lent them the structure they needed to develop their writing. In the years that followed, Miss Neussbaumn would loosen the requirements she imposed on her students that first year as she became more comfortable with the nontraditional style of teaching required by the writing workshop. But that was small comfort to Cassie.

Still, Cassie benefited from the freedom Miss Neussbaumn allowed during silent reading time. For Cassie, this was the best part of the day, when she was allowed 15 uninterrupted minutes with a book of her choice. Miss Neussbaumn's classroom had a small library of Newbery winners, and Cassie eagerly read *Roll of Thunder Hear My Cry* by Taylor and *Shiloh* by Naylor. When everyone else in class was reading Harry Potter books, she read and was utterly charmed by Sachar's *Holes*. The style of the writing intrigued her. She loved how the basic reality of the story was touched by a magical quality or event. Cassie wanted to read other books in that style so that she could include the same elements in her own stories. She discovered the style was called magic realism (Faris, 1995), and she asked her mother for other books in that style. Mrs. Bright was skeptical. She kept a close eye on what Cassie read to make sure that the themes were not too adult or too tragic. She and Cassie decided that she would read *Moon Lake* by Eudora Welty and *The Monkey* by Isak Dinesen and then write a short story in that genre. Cassie wrote the story over a weekend. The plot described a classroom of rowdy, bored students and what happened when Benjamin Franklin replaced their regular teacher. Typical of magical realism, the students simply accepted the new teacher without question and began a quest of learning as Franklin shared his special talents and knowledge with the students. In science class, the students studied how electricity was captured by a kite and a key, examined how a lightening rod worked, and investigated how to build a working battery. During a study of American history and the American Revolution, the students wrote their own Declaration of Independence. The students also created a classroom almanac in which each contributed an essay of classroom virtues and wisdom. When the course of study was completed, Franklin left as suddenly as he had appeared to be replaced by their regular teacher. The students continued in their ordinary studies but often convinced their teacher to try different approaches and investigations à la Franklin. Cassie presented the story to Miss Neussbaumn without prewriting or rough drafts.

What do you think Miss Neussbaumn's response will be? Will she be angry with Cassie? What do you think about Miss Neussbaumn's methods? What will happen between her and Cassie?

Your responses:

____

____

CASE STUDY TWELVE—INAPPROPRIATE SCAFFOLDING: CASSIE BRIGHT (PART II)

> Later that week, Miss Neussbaumn told her class that she was required to bring a sample of her students' writing to her class at the university to discuss. She asked if she could bring Will's, Cassie's, and one other girl's stories. The students all proudly agreed. Later that week, after her class had met, Miss Neussbaumn asked to conference with Cassie about her story. She told her that the other teachers and her instructor had been so impressed with Cassie's writing that they suggested she enroll in a summer camp for young writers sponsored by the university. If Cassie's mom couldn't afford the tuition, they would arrange for a scholarship. In the meantime, Miss Neussbaumn told Carrie, "I realize now what I have missed in looking at your writing. I promise in the future I will try to understand and to help you." Cassie's heart bounced with happiness.

How do you view Miss Neussbaumn's sudden change of attitude toward Cassie's writing? Would you expect that, with increased experience in the new writing instruction, Miss Neussbaumn would grow in her understanding of how to work with students at different levels of writing skill? Do you view this type of writing instruction as effective and beneficial to students or do you value more traditional writing instruction?

Your responses:

Evidencing the use of a reflective problem-solving approach—if you were able to discuss the implementation of Miss Neussbaumn's instructional methods and how her use of scaffolding stifled Cassie's progress rather than supporting the development of her talent
Evidencing an emerging use of a reflective problem-solving approach—if you agree in theory that all students should have instruction tailored to their special needs but argue that in reality this is impossible to accomplish—impossible because teachers have so many students to deal with, and they all can't receive specialized attention. In any case, students like Cassie are smart enough to learn on their own and don't really require special assistance from the teacher.
Evidencing the need for a reflective problem-solving approach—if you concluded that Cassie should simply follow instruction and do as her teacher says rather than whining and complaining in order to get special treatment. Teachers have little time to devote to the special needs of individual students, particularly high-achieving students. In this view, school is designed for the convenience of the teacher and not based on the needs of a variety of students.

CASE STUDY THIRTEEN—MISMATCHED ASSESSMENT METHODS: MATH TEACHER (PART I)

Denita Gregory was in her third year of teaching and was having an exceedingly difficult year. Although during the last two years Denita hadn't been thrilled with her teaching, this year her high school had changed to block scheduling, and she was really struggling. Her math students were not completing assignments, they refused to participate in class discussions, they came to class unprepared, and they were bored, distracted, and disinterested. And their behavior was getting increasingly difficult to control. Denita knew that part of the problem was the 90-minute class period; the students had trouble sitting still for so long. In the previous years, her periods were only 50 minutes long, and the extra 40 minutes was stretching her instructional skills to the limit.

Denita's school district was quite poor, so when they changed to block scheduling there hadn't been money for teacher professional development. The teachers were left to their own devices to figure out how to use the extra instructional time. Some of the teachers simply doubled up their lesson plans, but Denita had found that her students became confused with the increased amount of material. Rather than learning twice as much material, they didn't seem be learning anything at all. Next, Denita tried what other teachers suggested, which was to teach one lesson and then allow the students to complete their homework during class time rather than taking it home. Most of the time they actually completed their homework, and she was available if they had questions and could provide extra help for those who needed it. But still the students were bored and unmotivated, and, increasingly, the 40-minute homework session turned into a gossiping, napping, and horsing-around session.

Denita had always used rewards to motivate students to behave and to participate in learning. She offered special privileges such as using the computer, reward days with a movie and popcorn, candy, special field trips, praise, and the students' favorite, Coke breaks. A Coke break meant that, during the student's free time, he or she was allowed to go to the student break room and have a Coke on the school district. The students participated enthusiastically in the rewards, but Denita found the rewards tended to win her only temporary compliance. Ultimately, the rewards did not improve student behavior or promote learning. She also used punishment for unacceptable behavior, such as being disrespectful or horsing around, with the loss of a Coke break or calling parents to report the offense. The punishment brought even more immediate compliance, but students were then angry and resentful and covertly resisted her subsequent requests.

Denita's instructional methods were traditional and teacher centered. She lectured and presented examples on the board of the problems she wanted her students to practice for their homework. Sometimes she allowed students to work problems on the board. Sometimes they played competitive games. Her assessment methods were limited to paper and pencil tests of the same problems they had covered in the class and in homework. Even the best math students appeared bored with the routine. By the end of the school year, Denita was desperate to change her teaching.

Denita was an African American woman who had gone back to school to become a teacher after her own children were enrolled in school. Having children of her own had made her realize the importance of schooling and the advantage and happiness that a good education could provide children. She wanted to provide that goodness to all her math students. Denita had grown up in a strict home where she went to Sunday school and church every Sunday and Wednesday. She was expected to follow the rules at home and at school. Her parents expected her to do well in school and encouraged her to always try her best. She wanted that for her own students. She liked structure, so she organized her classroom with teacher-centered traditional methods and behavioristic classroom management.

During the summer, as Denita struggled with the problem of what to do with the 90-minute period, she also enrolled in a graduate class. This class also caused Denita to question her instructional techniques. One of the course requirements was for each teacher to analyze their teaching methods and report them to the group. In reviewing her teaching, Denita realized that, according to the textbook and discussions, she had been encouraging her students to adopt performance goals (Slavin, 2003). Performance goals direct students to concern themselves with grades and their performance on tests. It is a competitive system, with each student knowing how they stand in relationship to others in the class. When the teacher administers rewards and punishments, this is done publicly. Assessment procedures assume that if a student can pass a test, they understand and will retain the material. Denita came to realize that her use of multiple choice and the other traditional tests led her students to believe that their test performance verified their math ability. That is, if they performed well on the tests, they were talented in math, and if they didn't perform well, it was because they lacked innate math ability. Therefore, if students got behind or didn't understand a concept, they stopped trying because there was no reason to believe they could improve their skills.

Those students then began to come to class unprepared and made minimal effort on homework and tests. This also explained why they didn't participate in class activities or discussions; they didn't feel that they had anything to contribute. Denita began to conclude that her teaching methods were inhibiting her students' learning.

From her graduate course, Denita learned that the alternative to performance goals was learning goals. In this view of motivation, the teacher decreases emphasis on testing and increases focus on meaningful learning (Slavin, 2003), that is, learning that is meaningful to the students and addresses problems that students find interesting. Denita discovered that students who adopt learning goals are more focused on learning content and skills and less focused on testing and grades. They were also better problem solvers and used better learning strategies than performance goals students, and they were also more persistent in their learning. Learning goals students, when faced with obstacles to their learning, were more likely to view them as challenges that they needed to overcome.

When performance goal students are faced with poor grades or learning difficulties, they tend to give up or resort to cheating or other methods in order to save face with peers. To a performance goal student, a poor grade means that something is wrong with them and their ability to learn. These students claim what math teachers hear all too often: "I can't learn math, I'm not good at it." Denita's teaching played right into that student mentality. Now she was fully convinced that she wanted to change her teaching, but she wasn't sure how to start.

She decided she first had to change the way she presented mathematics. Rather than simply putting problems on the board and demonstrating how to work them, Denita had to present a context for the application of the mathematics that was interesting to the students. She combed through her math textbooks to find problem-solving applications for each of her topics. She also decided that she would use cooperative learning techniques so that students would learn to be responsible for helping each other to learn rather than compete over who got a Coke break that day. She decided she would identify three cooperative learning techniques that she would use routinely. She would also create hands-on problem-solving activities in which students measured and collected data to calculate and analyze, using the mathematics of her core curriculum.

Denita was not the kind of teacher to go into a classroom and attempt to "wing it"; she would begin the school year with a plan. To do this, she mapped all the mathematical topics she would need to cover on a grid. In one column she put the context and application of the problem, in the next she named the hands-on activity, and in the final column she listed the cooperative learning technique she would use. She challenged herself to use different techniques for each topic including think/share/pair, numbed heads together, and jigsaw. She didn't want her students to fall into a boring routine again. She wanted to make sure she was changing up the instructional methods for her students on each topic. Completing the grid was extremely challenging, but when she was finished, she was elated and couldn't wait to begin the school year. With the additional time required for the hands-on activities and cooperative learning groups, she was sure the 90-minute periods would be perfect.

The only aspect of her teaching that she wasn't willing to change was her traditional assessment methods. She would limit the amount of homework her students would complete, but she would still require pencil and paper quizzes each week, taken from the textbook, and administer midterm and final comprehensive exams.

The first of the school year produced for Denita an extended period of student whining, confusion, resistance, and constant questions (to make sure what they were doing was right). Denita thought she would lose her mind. She worked hard to reassure her teacher-dependent students that they could explore mathematical ideas on their own. The students also resented the loss of the Coke break and other rewards, but Denita was certain that she no longer wanted to bribe her students into learning.

Eventually, the students began to respond positively to her new teaching methods, and slowly they began to express more interest and take responsibility for their learning. One by one they began to come to class prepared and willing to work on assignments in a personally satisfying manner. Most of the students were eventually engaged in learning, but a problem surfaced. The one thing that Denita had refused to change—her testing methods—was undermining her new teaching strategies. Students who had become excited, interested, and involved in course projects reverted back to their dependent selves on testing days. They asked Denita over and over what would be on the test, what they would need to memorize, and if partial credit would be given for partially correct answers. On test days the students began to act like their former selves, and Denita wondered why this was happening. This time for help, Denita went to the course instructor of her graduate class. She showed her the grid, told her what she had attempted to do, and described how on testing days students seemed to lose ground in their quest to become independent learners and problem solvers.

What do you think is causing Denita's problem? What do you think the course instructor will tell her? What would you do?

Your responses:

___

___

___

___

CASE STUDY THIRTEEN—MISMATCHED ASSESSMENT METHODS: MATH TEACHER (PART II)

After Denita explained what she had attempted with her teaching, her instructor asked why she hadn't also changed her assessment methods. Denita said that she was worried about changing too much of her teaching at one time, and because grading was one of the most important ways she communicated with parents and others outside of her class, she was reluctant to "rock the boat" in her very conservative school. The instructor agreed that changing her assessment methods could create problems with parents, other teachers, and administration, but not changing them was creating problems for her students.

The instructor reminded Denita of class discussions about the power issues of the classroom and how teachers needed to be aware of their use of authority and how it determined the type of relationship she would have with her students (McEwan, 2000). It is to be expected of adolescents, as a part of their personality development, to challenge the authority of the teacher. How the teacher handles this challenge predicts the quality of student-teacher rapport. Denita was sending her students mixed messages about the type of power relationship that she wanted to have with her students. On one hand, during instruction, Denita communicated to students by permitting choices, encouraging problem solving and presentation of their ideas as a testimony that the knowledge they produced was meaningful and valuable. But through Denita's choice of testing methods she communicated that students should forget their ideas and their understanding of mathematics in order to regurgitate the teacher's knowledge on the test, that is, if they wanted to make a good grade. The instructor advised Denita that if she really wanted to make learning meaningful and student centered, she would also have to change how she assessed the students. She asked if Denita gave credit for the daily projects students completed in class or for their effort during the cooperative learning sessions. Denita said students didn't receive credit for any work other than their performance on homework quizzes and the exams. The instructor admonished Denita that assessment is where the "rubber meets the road," and it was through assessment and the awarding of grades that she was communicating what was truly important to her. There is a saying, "what is important gets assessed." By only assigning a grade for formal assessments, she was devaluing the class projects and the student effort that went into those projects. When she devalued their effort, thinking, and contribution, she also devalued her students.

The instructor asked how hard it would be for Denita to develop rubrics for the class projects and the cooperative activities so students could receive feedback on the effort and quality of their class projects and minimize the impact of quizzes and tests by lowering the amount of points they represented. She also recommended that Denita discuss this with her students before she made the change so they would understand what she wanted to accomplish through her assessment.

Denita protested that she had used a rubric once in the past but hadn't liked what happened. Denita explained that she had developed the rubric before the students worked on their project, but she was disappointed with the results so she changed the grading on the rubric to reflect what she had really expected. When the students discovered this, they had gotten angry, and a few parents had even called to protest their children's grade. After that, Denita didn't trust explaining her grading procedures because it allowed her students to question her grading. It was better to have tests that allowed only one right answer, then there could be no arguments. "Well, of course it caused trouble," explained the instructor. "You pulled a fast one on your students! The rubric promised them a grade for a certain quality of work, but then you changed the rules in the middle of the game and lowered their grade. You made a power move as the teacher that violated your students' trust. They expected that you would be fair in communicating your expectations for the assignment, and you were not. It's not the students' fault that you didn't communicate your expectations clearly from the first. Why should they pay for that with a lesser grade?"

The instructor explained to Denita that when she created a rubric, she felt obligated to stick with it no matter how disappointed she was with student responses. She simply changed the rubric for the next grading period, and, after a few changes, the rubric expressed what she wanted, and students knew what to expect from her on that project. Further, using scoring devices lets students know what to expect before they begin a project and thereby engenders trust between the student and teacher. This was particularly important for students who are overly anxious about their grades. The instructor finished by telling Denita not to be fearful. If she was serious about changing her teaching, she had to go all the way and change her assessment methods as well.

Denita felt hot and angry. She didn't say anything, but she thought it unfair that her instructor criticized her after all the effort she made to change her teaching. Nonetheless, by the time she left the building to walk to her car, Denita knew that she was going to include a new column on her curriculum grid that would list assessments for each topic.

What do you think about Denita's decision to change her teaching methods? How would you explain her resistance to also changing her assessment methods? What do you think is important to Denita as a teacher? Are these same values important to you?

Your responses:

____

____

____

____

Evidencing the use of a reflective problem-solving approach—if you were able to articulate the importance of the relationship between instruction and assessment and the manner in which assessments influence the power relationship between teacher

(Continued)

(Continued)

and students. Professional teachers are attuned to classroom power issues and how these can influence student learning.
Evidencing an emerging use of a reflective problem-solving approach—if you agree that Denita should change her teaching for the benefit of her students but think the student-teacher power issues are irrelevant. According to this view, students should simply do as they are told by the teacher and should not be concerned about their "rights" as students. In fact, power issues influence every classroom whether the teacher is aware of these or not.
Evidencing the need for a reflective problem-solving approach—if you believe that Denita should continue using the same instruction and assessments that she has always used. Because Denita teaches in a very conservative school, it would be in her best interest not to change but to teach and assess the same as the other teachers in the school. This view upholds the status quo even if it is in the best interest of the students and the teacher to change.

REFERENCES

Bracey, G. (2003). The 13th Bracey report on the condition of public education. *Phi Delta Kappan, 85*(2), 148–164.

Dixon-Krauss, L. (1996). *Vygotsky in the classroom.* White Plains, NY: Longman.

Faris, W. B. (1995). Scheherazade's children: Magic realism and postmodern fiction. In L. Parkinson Zamora & W. B. Faris (Eds.), *Magic realism* (pp. 163–190), Durham, NC: Duke University Press.

McEwan, B. (2000). *The art of classroom management.* Upper Saddle River, NJ: Prentice-Hall.

Rodgers, C. (2002). Defining reflection: Another look at John Dewey and reflective thinking. *Teachers College Record, 104*(4), 842–866.

Slavin, R. (2003). *Educational psychology.* Boston: Allyn and Bacon.

Solley, B. A. (2000). *Writers' workshop.* Boston: Allyn and Bacon.

Yopp, R. H., & Yopp, H. K. (2001). *Literature-based reading activities.* Boston: Allyn and Bacon.

INTERNET RESOURCES

Block Scheduling

www.jefflindsay.com/Block.shtml#intro
www.weac.org/resource/june96/schedule.htm

Block scheduling is a controversial topic in education. The first Web site presents a positive view of block scheduling. The second Web site is highly critical of this popular high school innovation.

Classroom Management

www.ez2bsaved.com/class_manage.htm

This site claims to provide the biggest and best collection of classroom management resources—a list of 694 sites.

Cooperative Learning

www.education-world.com/a_curr/curr287.shtml
www.sheridanc.on.ca/coop_learn/cooplrn.htm
http://college.hmco.com/education/pbl/tc/coop.html#top
http://muskingum.edu/~cal/database/group.html

These four Web sites explain the general benefits of cooperative learning techniques to support effective instruction. Detailed examples of specific techniques are available. Cooperative learning is one of the most researched instructional techniques, and its benefit for student learning, motivation, and the development of social skills is well documented.

High Stakes Assessment

www.naspcenter.org/factsheets/highstakes_fs.html
www.wrightslaw.com/info/highstak.index.htm

Both of these sites discuss issues of concern for students with special needs who are now held accountable for their learning progress in high-stakes systems. The most recent federal legislation, No Child Left Behind, includes special education students in the accountability pool. In the past, in many state systems, the achievement levels of students with individual educational programs (IEPs) were excluded from these tests. Some educators feel that it is proper to exclude special needs students, whereas others feel that they should be included so that schools will be held as accountable for their learning as students without identified disabilities.

www.reading.org/positions/high_stakes.html

The International Reading Association is an important and influential national group composed of teachers and teacher educators who teach reading. In this statement, the organization asserts its opposition to high-stakes assessment.

www.findarticles.com/cf_dls/m0JSD/11_57/77236967/p1/article.jhtml

Not every educator opposes high-stakes assessment. This Web site by a school administrator discusses the benefits and the liabilities of high-stakes assessment.

www.ed.gov/nclb/landing.jhtml?src=pb

This is the U. S. Department of Education's No Child Left Behind Web site. Interested readers can check out this legislated reform for themselves.

Reluctant Readers

www.glencoe.com/sec/teachingtoday/educationupclose.phtml/29
http://scholar.lib.vt.edu/ejournals/ALAN/winter94/Jones.html

Both of these Web sites offer suggestions to secondary teachers about how to help students who are struggling or reluctant readers.

www.reading.org/focus/struggling.html

The International Reading Association provides a page on its Web site to provide resources for struggling readers and writers.

Rubrics

http://rubistar.4teachers.org/index.php
http://edservices.aea7.k12.ia.us/framework/rubrics/index.html

Both of these Web sites provide practical information about rubric development for scoring student assignments.

Scaffolding Techniques

www.pugetsoundcenter.org/coaching_tools/profdev_scaffoldingt.html

Scaffolds are instructional support structures that teachers use to help students move to the next level in their learning. The targeted instructional level is work that students cannot complete independently but can accomplish with the help of a teacher or other support. This Web site discusses a variety of scaffolding techniques.

Vygotsky, Lev

www.education.miami.edu/blantonw/mainsite/Componentsfromclmer/Component13/Instruction/DialogicInquiryInEducation.html

An online paper about Vygotsky, the famous Russian psychologist, and the influence his work has had on education.

Writing Instruction

www.writingproject.org/

The Web site of the National Writing Project (NWP). The NWP supports the teaching of writing at all grade levels. It is recognized as one of the most successful and effective national programs for improving instruction. Most areas have a local version of the national project, where teachers receive training and resources for improving their writing instruction.

SEVEN

CASE STUDIES OF CLASSROOM AND SCHOOL CONTEXT

In this chapter, the case studies will explore problems of the classroom and school context. Context means the special qualities that make each classroom or school unique, such as age, race, ethnicity, gender, the values influence of parents and teachers, and the support of the community. Some educators view education as emerging from the particular context created by the vision of teachers, administrators, parents, and community members, whereas others view education as being imposed on students and the community by teachers and school administrators (Fullan, 2003). The following case studies assume that education flows from the community and individuals participating in the educational process. They also assume that the classroom teacher must genuinely consider classroom context when designing instruction.

These cases will present some of the most difficult and controversial problems attempted so far. In fact, the problems they present are sometimes determined to be unresolvable, because the issues are deeply rooted in people's beliefs, values, and convictions about school and society. When opposing value systems collide, the educational issue cannot be resolved without offending one system of values and the problem is therefore unresolvable (MacIntyre, 1984). Issues of race, class, gender, and religion often fall into this category and create extremely difficult classroom situations. Often teachers are not trained or do not expect to face such issues, and they may feel overwhelmed by the emotion, complexity, and difficulty of the decision-making process.

Common school controversies such as achievement tracking, special education services, and athletic and honors programs can often mask issues of race, class, gender, and religion. Often these situations are not considered proper conversation for polite society, and many teacher educators avoid them in professional courses for fear of hurting feelings or causing students to feel uncomfortable or even angry. In a diverse and democratic society such as the United States, it is common for parents and community members to attempt to gain control of a school's agenda in order to promote their own perspective or value system. Much of the argument one might witness at a school board meeting may result from individuals and groups jockeying for power within the school district. Much is at stake for parents because nothing is more precious than their children. When a teacher witnesses individuals who are particularly passionate about an issue, the teacher needs to ask himself or herself what is really at stake. Teachers need to consider the values that underlie the passion in order to understand the true nature of the problem.

For example, the elimination of an honors program and the resulting elimination of tracking may create outrage with the parents of honors students. Parents may feel that not only will the elimination of honors courses disadvantage their children in competition for good colleges and scholarships, but it will desegregate the student population. School tracking systems serve as de facto segregation systems when poor and minority students are disproportionably placed in the lower tracks. If such students are mixed into classes with high-achieving, privileged students, in the eyes of some parents, their children are being forced to fraternize with social riff raff. The honors students might even start to socialize with or date such "undesirables." Some social science researchers suggest that the tracking systems of schools not only reflect the social stratum of society but also serve to reinforce and maintain it. The school tends to act as a mirror of society, reflecting current values and issues that get played out in school board meetings and classrooms.

The next case study describes a more typical classroom context issue: a student who presents a classroom management problem for the teacher. The case study discussion describes in detail how to use a theory to analyze and solve a classroom problem. For each of the other case studies, you will use the reflective problem-solving process and the theory, research, and philosophy presented in previous chapters to determine solutions. The rubric at the end of each case study will provide feedback about your use of the reflective problem-solving process. The subsequent case studies in this chapter examine social class, race, and religion. The purpose of analyzing these case studies is not necessarily to solve the problem with one solution, but to practice using the reflective problem-solving process and to recognize and explore the complexities of the issues and to increase the reader's understanding before being confronted by these in a real classroom.

CASE STUDY FOURTEEN—DISRUPTIVE STUDENT: MORRIS LEONARD (PART I)

> Morris Leonard was a new student to the school and the district. He was slight with red hair and freckles. He dressed oddly with mismatched clothes that looked like they were from the department store bargain bin. But his clothes didn't seem to concern him, as he had one overriding passion in his life. His middle school social studies teacher claimed that he was one of the smartest individuals she had ever had in her class. Morris had an avid and overwhelming interest in history, particularly the Civil War era, to the extent that he could even refresh the teacher's memory on obscure points.
>
> Morris's grades were terrible in most subjects but were usually average in social studies. He absolutely refused to attempt any homework of any kind. He also ignored all tests except when the topic was of special interest to him, and then he invariably made a perfect score. If the topic was not interesting, he would turn in a blank test. Obviously, Morris's teacher was particularly frustrated by his work habits and the lack of achievement in such a bright and capable student, but the particular issue that Morris's teacher wanted to address was his wandering around the classroom. Morris had a habit of getting up and roving around the class at any time, during any activity. During study time, small group work, or even during a test, Morris would leave his seat to chat with other students, work on the classroom computer, open and lean out the window, or sit in a corner and chew on a pencil, spitting out pencil pieces on the floor. So far, the teacher had tried several approaches such as yelling at Morris, keeping him after school, writing notes to his parents, and sending him to the principal. Nothing seemed to work for long and soon Morris was up wandering around the classroom disturbing the rest of the class (the boys in class were particularly annoyed by this behavior and secretly called him a geek), not completing his work, and frustrating the teacher who felt he challenged her authority.

Given this description of Morris's behavior, what do you think is his problem? Once you have identified the problem, make sure the way you analyzed the problem fits the description of a reflective approach to problem solving.

Your responses:

____

____

____

____

CASE STUDY FOURTEEN—DISRUPTIVE STUDENT: MORRIS LEONARD (PART II)

In solving Morris's problem, remember that researchers have determined that reflective and nonreflective problem solvers are different in the quality of their problem solving at each stage, including problem identification (Ferry & Ross-Gordon, 1998). If we characterize yelling, after-school detention, notes home, and trips to the principal's office as punishments, how is Morris's teacher framing the problem? What does the teacher see as creating the problem? If the teacher is attempting to manage the classroom situation by punishing the student, is this reflective? What about your solution to the problem of Morris's wandering? Is your solution reflective? If we decide that punishing the student without understanding the reasons for the student's behavior is not reflective problem solving, let's consider more creative, reflective ways to view the situation. Reflective problem solving is based on the premise that having a more complete understanding of a complex problem will lead to more satisfactory solutions. To solve the problem reflectively and not just punish the student, the teacher needs to investigate what is creating the problem or ask why Morris is wandering around the classroom. All human beings, even the youngest of children, are complex, and we therefore need to investigate Morris by looking at his past academic performance and history of behavior in the classroom, interviewing his current and previous teachers, talking with his parents, and even talking with him to see what insight he might have about his classroom behavior.

For example, to attempt to explain the problem, let's examine what self-determination theory (discussed in Chapter 4) can contribute to the problem of Morris's wandering. On the surface, the problem seems to be that Morris is not participating in the regular classroom activities and that he is not performing academically to his potential. Recall that self-determination theory specifies that the classroom learning environment must satisfy three student needs (Deci & Ryan 1998):

Competence—developing and exercising learning skills

Relatedness—affiliation with others

Autonomy—self-determination or choice

By examining the clues the case study provides, we can analyze these in relation to student needs and determine if Morris's teacher provides a classroom environment designed to meet them. The case study described Morris's excellent performance in history, yet poor performance in all other academic areas. On investigation of Morris's transcripts and permanent records, it was discovered that his grades in elementary school were above average. His teachers did note that he was somewhat immature compared to the other children and was teased and had a difficult time making friends. This promising academic beginning declined as Morris moved through the elementary program until, by the time he reached middle school, his grades had completely tanked. From the evidence of Morris's work in the social studies classroom and his past academic progress, it would seem that Morris should have no trouble passing the course; that is, if he should decide to do so. The level of instruction in the course seems appropriate, although possibly at too low a level of instruction for Morris. Therefore, competence according to self-determination theory is not an issue here.

The next need in self-determination theory, relatedness, means that the classroom provides a supportive social environment for students and that students can develop affiliations in the classroom, including the teacher. Are there any indications that Morris has difficulty relating to his teacher and peers? Yes, there are plenty. The teacher has already expressed frustration with Morris's behavior, his wandering around the classroom at will, and his lack of academic achievement. What do we know about how his peers view Morris? His elementary records noted that Morris had difficulty making friends. Morris is new to the school, and the other students have expressed annoyance with Morris and his wandering habit. This annoyance may mirror the teacher's frustration. Students, even at the middle school level, pick up cues from the teacher and reflect those in their treatment of peers. They may also be annoyed that Morris is "allowed" to break a class rule by wandering around the classroom and by using the class computer without permission. They may view Morris's wandering as an invasion of their privacy if he looks over their shoulders or breaks into their conversations. Middle school students would tend to be hostile to one who breaks class rules or otherwise takes privileges that are unearned. At this stage of social development, rules are important to adolescents, and their view of what is fair is that everyone is treated the same. The most obvious piece of evidence is that the other students call Morris a "geek." The use of this term for Morris shows that he is ostracized from the group and is a sure sign that he is not included in their social world.

In Chapter 1 we discussed a teacher named Vivian Paley who wrote books about her classroom experiences. In her book *The Boy Who Would Be a Helicopter,* she described a troubled student who exhibited the strange behavior of pretending to be a helicopter by rotating his arms (1990). You would expect that the other students would ridicule and ostracize him for his bizarre behavior, but as the teacher modeled sensitivity and understanding, the children accepted and attempted to help him. As the school year progressed, the troubled student became more comfortable and integrated into the social structure of the classroom.

This analysis of the case study indicates that one of Morris's problems is his lack of acceptance by the teacher and the other students in the class. This situation would have to be improved if the teacher truly wanted Morris to perform better in her classroom. One way to accomplish this would be for the teacher to consider Morris's talents as classroom assets. Morris's knowledge of history and the computer could become a resource to the class for developing papers and answering questions. If Morris's gifts and interests could be viewed as helpful instead of an annoyance, others might regard him more positively. The teacher could also tactfully attempt to facilitate friendships with Morris's peers by placing him in cooperative groups where he is likely to be accepted. This could lead to his participation in the classroom social network and acceptance by his peers.

The last element in self-determination theory, autonomy, describes the amount of choice students have in determining their activities related to learning. If Morris's teacher runs her classroom in a teacher-centered manner, there will be little autonomy or student choice. Self-determination theory asserts that Morris should be given latitude in selecting assignments and that he should get credit for what he knows and can accomplish rather than completing the routine assignments of the course. These routine class assignments may not be appropriate for Morris's level of academic attainment in history. Also, granting Morris some privileges in determining his assignments gives the teacher a bargaining chip to persuade him to complete assignments that he is less enthusiastic about but may be willing to complete if he is also allowed to work in his areas of interest.

Students like Morris who have narrow interests in one topic or discipline can be frustrating to teachers who believe that a well-rounded education is important. Teachers want to see good effort in all the core subjects, but Morris has at least one interest for the teacher to build upon, and he could be encouraged to make connections to other areas based on that interest. Morris's problem can be contrasted with students who are completely withdrawn from school and exhibit no academic interests whatever. Morris has a place to begin to build connections to other academic areas. Flexibility in course assignments shouldn't be extended to just Morris with his obvious talent in history but to all the students in the class. Reviewing Figure 4.3 in Chapter 4 describing transmittal and constructivist classrooms, the active role of the student in the constructivist classroom is evident. The constructivist teacher values the individual views of students and expects that learning will be a different and personal experience for every student in the classroom.

Consider what effect you think these suggested changes might make on Morris's academic progress and, as a teacher, how comfortable you would feel with this type of flexibility and student freedom. Many teachers react, as did Morris's teacher, to classroom management problems by increased routine and regimentation of student behavior and curriculum. Both self-determination and constructivist theories would dispute that as a helpful classroom solution. Ultimately, every teacher must seek a balance between control and freedom for students and a satisfactory solution for students and teacher. What do you think about Morris's teacher's reaction to his challenge to her authority?

Your responses:

____

____

____

____

Evidencing the use of a reflective problem-solving approach—if you used the guidelines of self-determination theory or constructivist learning theory to suggest a plan to help Morris's teacher manage his behavior, improve his achievement, and interact more positively with the other students
Evidencing an emerging use of a reflective problem-solving approach—if you suggested a plan that would help Morris's teacher manage his behavior. This view addresses the symptoms of Morris's problem and improves the classroom for the teacher but fails to address the other educational difficulties that Morris faces.
Evidencing the need for a reflective problem-solving approach—if you suggested that the teacher should simply demand that Morris stay in his seat and punish him if he disobeys. This solution only treats the symptoms of Morris's difficulties. It fails to consider underlying causes for the misbehavior, risks escalating the problem behavior, and could further alienate Morris from the classroom and the teacher.

CASE STUDY FIFTEEN—BLACK/WHITE QUESTION: ENGLISH TEACHER

Skip Travers had just completed his student teaching, which he viewed as only moderately successful. Throughout his student-teaching semester he had been plagued by doubts as to whether he had anything to offer his students. The students hadn't seemed very interested in him or his ideas and he couldn't say that he blamed them. What did literature, poetry, and essay writing offer many of these students? He wasn't sure he had an answer. Now that he was searching for his first teaching position, he still wasn't sure. Skip was an English major, and even during a teacher shortage he couldn't find a position close to home, so he applied to urban areas where positions were always available.

He signed a contract with a school district 300 miles north of his hometown in an older suburban community that was slowly losing its enrollment. It had once been an affluent district, but much of the middle class was moving out and eroding its tax base. The previous generations had been committed to their community, which included several all-black middle class neighborhoods and many poorer integrated neighborhoods. Now this committed population was aging, and their children were moving out. The district consisted of several huge crumbling brick buildings with small numbers of students left to ramble around in them. The district population was diverse, with 45% white, 30% black, 10% Hispanic, and 5% more recent immigrants, including Asians and Eastern Europeans. The diversity worried Skip. He came from a small rural town where everyone was white and related to each other. Everyone went to the same school and attended either the West Side or East Side Baptist church. Skip knew what to expect from them because they all thought pretty much alike.

At his college there had been a few blacks and international students, but none that he had become friends with or had gotten to know. It wasn't that he didn't want to associate with more diverse friends, it was just that he continued to hang out with his hometown buddies. His education courses addressed diversity and dealing with students who represented a whole array of differences, but it all just made Skip nervous. Spina bifida, cerebral palsy, the hearing impaired, black, Asian, Latino, LD, BD, AD/HD, EMR—who could deal with all of those differences in people? Skip didn't even want to think about it, so he didn't ask any pertinent questions during his interview.

Skip was assigned to teach freshman composition, honors English, and world literature. He also agreed to coach soccer, a sport that he had played in high school and college, but which he had no idea how to coach. When Skip met with his classes for the first time, he found that each included blacks and Latino students along with the white kids, except for the honors English class, where everyone was white. No spina bifida, thank goodness! In the first few weeks, he felt excruciatingly uncomfortable and self-conscious in front of his students. He was a fraud, not a real teacher at all, and soon the students would discover it. He worried about his accent, wondering if they considered him a hick. But other than asking him if he was from around here and then laughing, they didn't seem interested in him at all. They also didn't seem to expect much from him.

He read "good" literature to them and he assigned readings and papers that sometimes they completed and other times ignored. He put them into groups to work on projects because he had been taught in his education courses that this was an educationally sound practice. Soon he discovered that he enjoyed watching them work together, how they interacted and how they treated each other. He noticed the boys and girls attempting to flirt with each other. He witnessed attempted seductions and failed romances with occasional tears and angry sarcasm. He slowly began to use that sexual tension to help relate classic literature to their lives. He emphasized Romeo and Juliet as a young couple in love against the backdrop of gang violence. It was a perfect fit for the urban setting of his school. Of course he showed West Side Story (they laughed at the "menace" of the Sharks and Jets) and the Claire Danes and Leonardo DiCaprio film version of the play.

Watching his students and thinking about them helped to lessen his self-consciousness. He found that, when he was thinking about them, he didn't think so much about himself. And he learned from watching them. He was particularly interested in how the boys interacted and joked with each other, because he had to deal with them as both coach and teacher. He always made sure his groups were very diverse; he wanted to see how they got along. They related surprisingly well—which amazed him. Where he had expected racial tension he found little. Well, except for when the Latino girls flirted with the white and black boys. The Latino guys really got mad at "their" girls when they caught them. But for the most part all the guys got along fine, and he realized from talking with them after school and during practice that they had known each other all their lives. They had grown up in integrated neighborhoods where they played ball and rode bikes together. Skip expected to see racial tension, and he knew all about racism: He had grown up with it in his little southern town. Racial slurs and jokes were common. His uncle was one of the town's most notorious bigots. He didn't understand his own motivation or what had made him want to think differently. He didn't know what made him shrink from the values of his cousins and his brothers. He simply knew that he wanted to understand other kinds of people and live a life different from his parents'.

He worried about what he was teaching his students. The curriculum was traditional and included the canon of literature, grammar, essay writing, and research reports. He wondered if he should make his instruction more multicultural, the way he had been taught in college. He wondered what would happen if he related his instruction more to the students' lives, if this would make it more meaningful to them? They seemed to be sleepwalking through their education, and no one cared. Did he dare to wake them up? How would he do that?

Skip listened to the boys as they talked in the hall or the locker room. Their language in the halls was different from what they used in the classroom. He had expected great differences between the dialects of the blacks and whites, but he didn't hear it. In the classroom, both groups expressed equally atrocious spoken and written grammar while, outside the classroom, the language spoken was a dialect used by both the blacks and whites. It sounded a lot like "yo yo" this and "yo yo" that to Skip. It included lots of hand slapping and jostling, insults and jokes. Should he explore the use of that dialect? Should he encourage his students to write in their own language? Would that inspire them to go beyond the boring, simple, poorly constructed, thoughtless writing they typically turned in? He didn't know.

He tried talking with the other English teacher, Millie Charleston, after school. She advised him to teach the district's basic curriculum, because the district's achievement scores were atrocious and if anyone cared enough to look they would shut them down. Skip asked about purchasing reading materials that were relevant to the students' lives, but Mrs. Charleston snapped that there was no money in the budget for additional supplies or books. Skip would have to teach with what he had. She advised Skip, "We do what we can for these kids, but don't you expect too much of them." On that hostile note, she quickly got her things and left. She wasn't interested in chitchat after school, and she always left before it got dark. She was in a hurry to get home to her husband and her cats.

Disgusted, Skip decided that he would talk to the principal about the budget anyway. He would ask for trade books that were more contemporary and culturally diverse. The only book on the district list written by an African American or even written about the African American experience was *Go Tell It on the Mountain* by James Baldwin. Even the world literature text was dull. None of the short stories seemed to spark interest or discussion with his students.

The principal was an African American, and Skip knew that he had lived in the district all of his life. Given this experience, Skip reasoned that the principal would understand his students' cultural experiences. Skip envisioned teaching in a way that related to the students' cultural experiences and engaging the students with activities that transformed their lives and made them regard him as a special force in their lives. Right now he simply had no clue what those experiences were or how to begin. On the day of the meeting, the principal shook Skip's hand and asked how things were going. Skip said they were OK and asked if he could purchase material that would relate to his students' experiences. Was there any money? The principal said that the budget was tight, but if Skip would give him purchase orders for materials he would order them in the spring with carryover funds. Next spring! thought Skip. Skip asked if the principal had ideas about how to relate to the students' experiences because he had been in the district and the community for so many years. The principal replied that Skip should to talk with Mrs. Charleston; she was a good resource and she had taught English for a long time. Yeah, thought Skip, thanks a lot.

Skip didn't know who to talk with next, but he considered the school counselor, Lenny Heard. The counselor was also an African American, and Skip thought he looked pretty cool with his dreadlocks and nice suites and ties. Skip also observed that he related well with the students, but Skip felt shy about approaching him. What would Skip say? An opportunity came after the first football game of the season. The counselor announced the game, and he and all of the coaches went to the local pub for a beer after the game. The other guys had left, and it was just Skip and the counselor. Skip explained that he had noticed how well the counselor got along with the kids, especially the black students, and asked if he had any advice about what he should do with his classes? Lenny looked disgusted and retorted, "You think just because I'm a black man,

I understand all things African American?" Skip had been worried about this particular reaction. He knew from his college studies that it could be interpreted as an insult to ask a minority person to represent an opinion for the entire group. The African American community was diverse, and no one person could represent a unified response. Skip apologized, "No, no that's not what I meant. It's just that I need help, and I don't know who to ask. I already talked with Mrs. Charleston and then the principal and now you the counselor." "Well, I understand that. It must have been discouraging to talk to those two retirees," replied the counselor. "I'm working on my doctorate so it happens I've done some research on desegregation issues and the black-white achievement gap. I can tell you what I know." The two had a few more beers and talked for several hours.

Then Lenny described something that surprised Skip. He asked if Skip knew about the doll study. One of the most compelling pieces of evidence examined by the U.S. Supreme Court during *Brown v. Board of Education of Topeka* was the doll study. The study was conducted in 1939 with 253 African American children, ages 3–7. The children were asked to select their preference for a doll that could be either black or white. A major conclusion of the study was that the children's selection of the white doll demonstrated a preference for white skin and an indication of negative attitude toward the children's own racial identity. Years later the court viewed negative personal identity as a primary cause of school failure among African American students and felt that this could best be remedied by the desegregation of schools (Marshall, 2002). The study was hotly debated for years, and other doll studies were conducted with mixed results, but a researcher who examined the same data years later found that the original researchers had collected, but not reported, data that actually demonstrated a preference by 7-year-olds for the black doll (Marshall, 2002).

Lenny continued talking and asked if Skip realized that a significant gap existed between black and white achievement test scores, which had persisted for decades and which no one could adequately explain (Jencks & Phillips, 1998). Researchers discovered that when black children entered school they scored significantly lower on achievement tests compared to white children. They knew that this achievement gap persisted throughout the school years and beyond despite efforts to narrow it (Jencks & Phillips, 1998). Researchers theorized that the initial gap was influenced by a wide variety of factors, including social environment, parenting skills, and the mother's level of education. But researchers also noted that teachers' influence on student achievement could also contribute to the gap. Investigators had found that teachers were good predictors of students' future performance based on their observations of students' current classroom abilities (Ferguson, 1998). Teacher expectations also influenced students' perceptions of their abilities. Most surprising was the finding that this teacher effect is more significant for black students than it is for white students. For example, one study asked eighth and ninth graders who they most wanted to please with their schoolwork. "Teachers" was the answer for 81% of black females, 62% of black males, 32% of white males, and 28% of white females. White students were more concerned with pleasing their parents (Casteel, 1997).

The practical consequence of this was the need for teachers to realize the important effect their expectations could have on students, particularly African American students. If teachers effectively communicated their expectations of student performance based solely on observed test results, teachers would necessarily communicate lower expectations for black students based on their low initial scores. So although society's expectation that achievement deficits demonstrated when black students entered school would be improved by education, this outcome wouldn't be achieved if teachers regularly communicated low expectations for these students.

The remedy for this predicted "teacher effect" is for teachers to be more responsive to children's progress and efforts to improve and for teachers to be less judgmental about initial low test results. Teachers need to remain realistic but positive in their belief that all students can achieve academically, and they need to communicate this optimism to their students. Teachers can also use a variety of instructional techniques that have proven effective for all students but that have particularly positive effects on black and other low-achieving students (Ferguson, 1998).

One such technique is the use of an extended "wait time." Wait time is the time delay after the teacher asks a question before he or she calls on a student to answer. Longer wait time encourages females, low-achieving students, and minority students to participate in classroom discussions and improves classroom performance (Rowe, 1987). Providing corrective neutral feedback to students is also effective in improving student performance. This technique provides students with correction for mistakes and feedback on how to improve their performance. Teachers should also emphasize cooperation rather than competition in the classroom as a way to encourage students to be responsible for the success of the entire classroom, not just the success of a few "winners." In addition, teachers can use a curriculum that is sensitive to the culture of the community and to the needs and interests of the students. Therefore, rather than using prepackaged curriculum and relying on textbooks to plan instruction, teachers should construct their own curriculum designed to engage and excite the interest of their students (Marshall, 2002). Again, although all of these methods have proven helpful to all types of students, their benefits are disproportionately significant and positive for minority students.

As they walked out of the pub, Lenny ended his advice to Skip by saying, "So while the good news is you don't have to do anything different or special for the African American kids, you are going to have to get your rear in gear and improve your teaching for all the kids. I'll talk to the principal about getting you your new books."

Do you believe the counselor's advice that all students benefit from the same effective instructional methods, or do you believe that blacks and other minorities need special teaching methods? Do you think that literature more representative of his students would help to inspire Skip's students? Does the classroom teacher have a responsibility for narrowing the black/white achievement gap? Or do you believe home and community are the deciding factors in student achievement?

What would you suggest as a plan for Skip to improve his teaching? What are your biggest fears related to teaching minority students?

Your responses:

____

____

____

____

Evidencing the use of a reflective problem-solving approach—if you used the evidence about black and white student achievement and "teacher effects" derived from research to describe a plan to permit Skip to improve his teaching.
Evidencing an emerging use of a reflective problem-solving approach—if you developed a plan for Skip to improve his teaching but didn't use theory or research as the framework for the plan, but rather used your own experiences and knowledge to base the plan.
Evidencing the need for a reflective problem-solving approach—if you don't think Skip should change his teaching because schools with poor and minority students have little chance of overcoming the negative influences of home and community. This is a status quo view of education that ignores research that demonstrates, with the proper support, poor and minority students can achieve.

CASE STUDY SIXTEEN—CULTURAL CONTACT: CINDI SKILLMAN

Cindi Skillman is a 15-year-old white female and a sophomore attending a small Catholic girls school. Cindi wears thick glasses and has a wide gap between her two front teeth. She is of average height but is slightly overweight, and her body appears flabby and out of shape. Cindi has a very fair complexion, and her long hair is fine and mousy brown. Her family enrolled her in a religious school because they wanted Cindi to receive a Catholic education, but Cindi struggles to make passing grades in most of her classes. Cindi's family lives in the small, low-income, working-class community of

Johnerville. Johnerville is located some distance from the school on the outskirts of the large, rather wealthy community of St. Anne. Students from Johnerville were called Johnervillers by the St. Anne students. They ride a county bus to and from school, causing them to leave their classes early. Cindi's family consists of her mother, little sister, and maternal grandmother. Her father has never been a part of her life. Her mom supports the family, but she has recently lost her job at the local grocery store and is now working in the school's cafeteria.

Cindi doesn't have any close friends at school. She hangs on the fringes of groups of girls as they socialize, and she bids for their attention. If Cindi interjects herself in their conversation, she is impatiently heard but her contribution is ignored, and the girls roll their eyes and make mocking faces behind her back. Cindi doesn't speak or dress like the other girls. She has a distinct Johnerville accent that is more nasal and rural than the mall talk dialect that other girls effect. Cindi's clothes are never in accord with the other girls who shop endlessly at the mall and who follow specific adolescent fashion trends that change subtly and often. Cindi attempts to follow the trends but falls a year behind with shoes and 6 months behind with jeans and backpacks. Even when Cindi wears the "right" clothes, she never achieves the same look as the other girls, and they punish her for not fitting in and for even presuming that she be included in their groups.

To the new history teacher, Michael Calcagno, the girls seem cruel, but he also recognizes that Cindi contributes to her own problem. He learned about Cindi and her issues from the other teachers right after school began. In the recent past, Cindi had been included in various groups by some of the girls. For reasons that baffle Michael, Cindi developed a destructive pattern of behavior that invariably costs her a place in the group. Cindi would finally manage to establish a tenuous connection with a small group of girls who allowed her the privilege of eating lunch and socializing with them between classes when Cindi would create a social disaster by telling a large, very damaging lie to the others in the group regarding one of the girls. This effectively ostracized her from the group, because even though this type of social blackmail was used by the other girls, Cindy's status in the group was much too low to allow her to utilize this technique for gaining attention.

After each of these incidents, Cindi would go to her teachers and "plead her case," hoping that one of the teachers would take pity on her and "save" her from the condemnation of the female group. At first, the teachers were marginally sympathetic to Cindi, but as they noticed the incident being repeated, they began to avoid Cindi and her efforts to engage them on her behalf.

Michael remained loyal to Cindi's cause and attempted to help Cindi affiliate with the other students. He often used group work during instruction and activities. He carefully selected groups, hoping to help Cindi by including her in a group where she might be supported and connect with a friend. When students were paired for projects he made sure Cindi's partner was one of the kinder, less status-conscious girls. All of his efforts seemed to be to no avail. Cindi continued to be socially aggressive, and the more she pushed herself on others the more they repelled her. They wouldn't do it in front of Michael, but he would sometimes overhear biting comments directed toward Cindi or catch glimpses of the shunning behavior meant to communicate to Cindi that she had nothing to contribute and would never belong. Things were worse when Cindi's mother began working in the cafeteria. Her mother adored Cindi, and as she heaped extra helpings of the school lunch on her plate, the "wanna-be" anorexic girls giggled and made sly comments about Cindi's weight.

After a while Michael started to agree with the other teachers that Cindi's need for attention and social approval was overwhelming and interfering with her learning. Teachers and students viewed her as a "drama queen." It always seemed that academics were put on the back burner until some social crisis was resolved. At the same time, Michael had sympathy for this outsider. In his view, the teachers seemed to be in collusion with the students who were socially ostracizing Cindi for being who she was—a girl from the working class who was not like them. Not being from the area himself, he didn't hold the same prejudice against Johnerville nor the same snobby high regard for St. Anne. In his view, the students were not as brilliant and accomplished as they thought they were.

Housing in St. Anne was overpriced, and he couldn't afford to live in the community where he worked but commuted 30 minutes. He often felt like an outsider himself in the close-knit community with its subtle speech, behavior, and dress codes. He had a particular plaid tie that he would never wear again after the female teachers giggled and joked about it for a week. He considered having a conversation with Cindi's mother about sending her to the local public school where Cindi might have a better chance of establishing friendships and be freed from the relentless struggle to fit into social groups where she would never belong.

What do you think about Michael Calcagno's assessment of Cindi's situation? Could the social aspects of her life create such turmoil that Cindi is unable to learn? What about the school and teachers? Do you think teachers make judgments about students based on social class and popularity with the other students? Do feel the teachers are in collusion with the students to make Cindi feel unwelcome? Does it matter that the school is private, not public? What is the responsibility of teachers to students who are socially unattractive?

Your responses:

____

____

____

____

Evidencing the use of a reflective problem-solving approach—if you suggested that Mr. Calcagno hold a discussion with Cindi, her mother, her teachers, and the administrators of the school to determine how the school could change so that Cindi would have an opportunity to become academically successful and socially accepted at the school.
Evidencing an emerging use of a reflective problem-solving approach— if you suggested that Mr. Calcagno hold a discussion with Cindi, her mother, her teachers, and the administrators of the school to determine how Cindi

(Continued)

(Continued)

could change to be more academically successful and socially accepted at the school.
Evidencing the need for a reflective problem-solving approach—if you suggested that the school's administration should ask both Cindi and Mr. Calcagno to leave and find another school because neither of them "fit" at the school. This is a status quo view of schooling that assumes teachers, students, and parents should conform to the bureaucracy of the school rather than the school making changes to accommodate the members of the school community.

CASE STUDY SEVENTEEN—CLASSROOM HOLIDAY DECORATIONS: ELEMENTARY TEACHER

Nigella Dupre had finally landed her dream job in the Sheridan school district, a large growing district in an affluent suburb. The community included not only a large university but an international software company as well. Its population was diverse, affluent, and well educated. Nigella had worked in several small, poor systems and she was tired of large class sizes, running out of construction paper in the middle of the school year, sharing books, and begging to use the copy machine. The Sheridan district paid better than surrounding districts, the buildings were attractive, and new materials and resources were abundant. The diversity of the district was also attractive to Nigella. The district's population included wealthy African American, Asian American, Jewish, as well as Caucasian families. The district was happy to hire Nigella, a young, talented African American woman, and she was happy to be there.

Before classes started, Nigella brought boxes of materials from her old school to unpack and arrange in her new classroom. She glanced around the room to see how much storage it provided, as Nigella had accumulated a lot of materials, all of it bought with her own money. She was satisfied with the size of the built-in shelves and closets. The teacher from the next room dropped by and introduced herself as Sarah Whitacker and asked if Nigella needed help settling in. Nigella thanked her, and they proceeded to open boxes and chat as they got to know each other. Sarah asked if Nigella's momma was a poet because she certainly had a lyrical ear for names. Nigella laughed and said her brother's name was Donatella Dupre—Donny Dupre—for short, and they were shocked when he hadn't turn out to be a fashion designer. She explained that her brother was also a teacher and taught high school French back home in Louisiana.

Sarah remarked that Nigella had an amazing collection of materials to decorate her classroom. Nigella had clearly labeled boxes for each season, each holiday, and dozens of different topics and subjects. Nigella answered that she liked to frequently change the physical environment of her room to keep her students interested. One of the ways she celebrated the cycle of the school year was to have the students take down the old stuff and put up the new. Her previous principal had always brought visitors and prospective parents to her classroom because she had the most attractive and visually appealing room in the school. She also had many houseplants and a saltwater fish tank that she planned to bring later. Nigella explained that she used the fish tank to teach everything from science to language arts, and she was excited about the buzz the movie *Finding Nemo* was creating. She intended to exploit that theme for everything it was worth.

When Nigella and Sarah opened the box marked "Christmas," Sarah asked if the principal had talked to Nigella about the issue of Christmas at their school when he hired her. Nigella said she didn't know what she meant, and Sarah proceeded to tell her that because of the objections of the Jewish parents, no Christmas symbols were allowed in the school or the classrooms. Nigella was shocked: "No Christmas tree, no Santa Claus, no reindeer?" "Nope," said Sarah. "What about wreaths and bells?" "Nothing," replied Sarah. "The Jewish parents say their children are exposed to enough of that stuff at Christmas, and they shouldn't have to be surrounded by it at school. About the only decorations you can use during Christmas time are things related to cold weather like mittens and snowflakes." Nigella sat back on her heels, still surprised, and asked if she could have a Christmas tree if she included a menorah and Kwanzaa candles in the display. She had done that at her old school. "No way," said Sarah. "And nobody is fooled if you get a little Christmas tree and call it a Hanukkah bush." Nigella asked how the principal could allow this, and what did the Christian parents say? Sarah said, "The principal agrees with anything the parents want. In a school like this, the parents have a lot of power and they expect to get their way. The Christian parents who care about it send their kids to a private Christian school." Sarah asked to see Nigella's classroom roster. "Look," she said, "You have at least six Jewish kids. And you have two kids from Japan, but don't worry about them: The Buddhists are really laid back. Good thing you don't have a Jehovah Witness, then you couldn't carve pumpkins or send valentines!"

What do you think about this unexpected restriction? Do you think it is unfair to Nigella? What level of influence should parents have in a school? What do you think Nigella will do? What would you do?

Your responses:

____

____

____

____

Evidencing the use of a reflective problem-solving approach—if you suggested that Nigella should learn more about her students, the school, parents, and the community before she makes a decision about using the Christmas decorations. Time will tell if she can accept and fit into the diverse culture of the school.
Evidencing an emerging use of a reflective problem-solving approach—if you think Nigella should leave to find a school where her beliefs will be honored and supported. A person's beliefs are important, and they should not be compromised in order to remain a part of a group. This view only considers one side of the argument. The rights of the teacher are one side, but it ignores the rights of the students and families and fails to negotiate both sides of the controversy.
Evidencing the need for a reflective problem-solving approach—if you suggested that Nigella should use her Christmas decorations anyway. Her religious

beliefs are important to her and the children would benefit from a religious perspective, even if the parents don't agree with it. This view completely ignores the rights of students and their families.

REFERENCES

Casteel, C. (1997). Attitudes of African American and Caucasian eighth grade students about praise, rewards, and punishments. *Elementary School Guidance and Counseling, 31,* 262–272.

Deci, E. L., & Ryan, R. M. (1998). *Intrinsic motivation and self-determination in human behavior.* New York: Plenum.

Ferguson, R. F. (1998). Teachers' perceptions and expectations and the black-white test score gap. In C. Jencks & M. Phillips (Eds.), *The black-white test score gap* (pp. 273–317). Washington, DC: Brookings Institution Press.

Ferry, N. M., & Ross-Gordon, J. M. (1998). An inquiry into Schon's epistemology of practice: Exploring links between experience and reflective practice. *Adult Education Quarterly, 48*(2), 98–112.

Fullan, M. (2003). *The moral imperative of school leadership.* Thousand Oaks, CA: Corwin Press.

Jencks, C., & Phillips, M. (1998). The black-white test score gap: An introduction. In C. Jencks & M. Phillips (Eds.), *The black-white test score gap* (pp. 151–317). Washington, DC: Brookings Institution Press.

MacIntyre, A. (1984). *After virtue.* Notre Dame, IN: Notre Dame Press.

Marshall, P. L. (2002). *Cultural diversity in our schools.* Belmont, CA: Wadsworth.

Paley, V. (1990). *The boy who would be a helicopter.* Cambridge, MA: Harvard University Press.

Rowe, M. B. (1987). Wait time: Slowing down may be a way of speeding up. *American Educator, 11*(1), 38–43, 47.

INTERNET RESOURCES

Classroom Management

http://teachermentors.com/MCenter%20Site/ClMgmtTips.html

A list of classroom management tips for first-year teachers.

www.indiana.edu/%7Ecafs/tt/v1i2/what.html

This site provides an inventory that identifies classroom management profiles as authoritarian, laissez-faire, or indifferent.

Effective Instruction

http://muskingum.edu/~cal/database/genpurpose.html
http://edservices.aea7.k12.ia.us/framework/strategies/index.html
www.uncw.edu/cte/et/articles/bulger/
www.mcrel.org/topics/topics.asp?topicsid=6

These Web sites provide resources and information about instructional practices that have been found to be particularly effective for increasing student achievement.

Ethnic Diversity

http://teacher.scholastic.com/products/ect/placetobegin.htm
www.familyeducation.com/topic/front/0,1156,65–21926,00.htmlwww.waldorfhomeschoolers.com/diversity.htm

These Web sites provide general resources for teachers about how to present lessons in ethnic diversity.

www.naacp.org/
www.getnet.net/~1stbooks/
www.adl.org/adl.asp
http://nativeweb.org/

These additional Web sites provide specific information and resources for teachers about particular ethnic groups including African Americans, Hispanics, Jews, and Native Americans, respectively.

www.glsen.org/templates/index.html

The website of the Gay, Lesbian and Straight Education Network has a link for students and teachers and a library of resources.

Intrinsic Motivation Theory

http://comp.uark.edu/~brooks/motivational.html
www.motivation-and-motivational-tools.com/
http://education.calumet.purdue.edu/vockell/EdPsyBook/Edpsy5/Edpsy5_intrinsic.htm

These Web sites provide information about intrinsic motivation and how it is contrasted with extrinsic motivation.

Lesson Plans

www.AmericanTeachers.com/lessonplans.cfm#1423

This Web site offers lesson plans in many content areas and other resources for teachers.

www.mcrel.org/lesson-plans/index.asp

The Mid-Continent Research for Education and Learning (McREL) Web site also offers a collection of lesson plans for teachers.

Race and Educational Achievement

www.ncrel.org/gap/library/text/whatmatters.htm
www.rethinkingschools.org/archive/15_04/Race154.shtml
www.educationnext.org/20033/79.html

A number of online papers present a variety of perspectives on the difficult issue of race and school achievement.

Religion in Schools

www.ed.gov/policy/gen/guid/religionandschools/index.html

This Web site, from the U.S. Department of Education, provides guidelines for educators about religious expression and prayer in public schools. It is interesting to note how the No Child Left Behind legislation has changed the tone of these guidelines. Previously, students were "protected" from prayer in schools; now their rights to pray or not to pray are both protected.

Social Class and Education

www.trinity.edu/mkearl/strat.html
www.ericfacility.net/ericdigests/ed357433.html

Both of these short articles explore the relationship between school achievement and social class.

www.ncrel.org/gap/clark/factors.htm

This study of Nashville schools refutes the conventional wisdom that out-of-school factors such as race, class, and home environment play the primary role in school success. This study suggests that it is in-school factors that matter most.

PART IV

CREATING YOUR OWN CASE STUDY

EIGHT

DEVELOPING YOUR OWN CASE STUDY

REFLECTIVE CONSIDERATIONS

- Why should I develop my own case study?
- How do I develop a case study?
- Why is this important to me as a future teacher?

In this final chapter you will learn to develop your own case study in order to solve a student or classroom problem. You might wonder why, after spending considerable time analyzing the prepared case studies in this book, it is necessary to develop your own case study? The reason for developing your own case study is to provide the most authentic classroom problem-solving experience possible. The process is authentic in the sense that this is how reflective teachers solve their daily classroom problems.

Creating your own case study provides practice in using a formal process for solving individual student and classroom problems. Whether a teacher writes and solves case studies in the formal written manner described by this book or operates in a more informal manner and solves problems mentally, the process is essentially the same. Internalizing the problem-solving process and using it regularly will allow the reader to incrementally improve and refine teaching practices. Incremental improvement will move the reader more quickly to becoming a professional teacher. As challenging and engaging as the case studies in this book have been, it is particularly meaningful to identify and solve one's own problems. Recalling the swimmer's metaphor from Chapter 4, this is where you truly begin to develop your swimmer's muscles.

Before you begin to select a problem and develop a case study, let us first review the process of the case study method. So far, we have examined the meaning of reflection and its importance in becoming an effective teacher. We have investigated the contents of reflection including philosophy, theory, research, and the subject matter needed to make informed and professional decisions. You have practiced problem solving using prepared case studies. Now, in this final step, you will identify, describe, analyze, and solve your own case study. This book presents a fully scaffolded problem-solving process from building an understanding of reflection to analysis of example case studies to the design and solution of one's own problem.

Following is the outline you will use to develop the case study. The case study design process has many sections, and in each section instruction and examples are provided so the writer may develop his or her problem in a step-by-step manner.

Process of Case Study Development

I. Selecting a case
   a. ethical considerations
II. Describing the case
   a. clear unbiased description
   b. use of descriptive data
   c. withholding judgment
III. Problem identification
IV. Solution generation
V. Reflecting on the solution

PROCESS OF CASE STUDY DEVELOPMENT

Selecting a Case Study Problem

When developing a case study, the first consideration is to select a problem that is interesting or important to you. Because you are going to spend several hours working on this task, it is important to select a topic or a student that will make the project worthwhile and meaningful. You may select a topic because you know someone who has an educational problem that distresses you, or you may want to obtain more knowledge about a difficulty. For example, you may have a sibling, a child, or a friend with special educational needs that you would like to understand better. Often students who aspire to become teachers are inspired by their experiences helping others or observing a situation where an educational need has not been addressed. You might want to design a case study about an individual who has a developmental disability, a learning disability, or limited English proficiency or a student who is not achieving properly. You may also be inspired by your own experiences as a learner. You may remember a teacher who had poor classroom management or instructional skills, and you have vowed never to allow that to happen to you as a teacher. Whatever you decide, the case study is a way to help you understand the situation or the individual in a detailed manner. It will also prepare you to address a similar problem in the future.

Ideally, you should be in a real teaching situation such as a field experience, practicum, or student teaching when you design your case study because this will make the experience particularly meaningful and instructional. While observing in a busy classroom, it should be easy to identify a number of situations or problems you are interested in investigating. If you do not have the option of a live experience, you can rely on your memory of a past intriguing situation to design your case.

Following are a number of examples describing why students in my classes selected a particular child to investigate. You will notice that the students were all engaged, charmed, or otherwise enticed to select a particular child. You are looking for this same experience in your own selection, something that appeals to, draws, or moves you.

Example One. DeShawn is one of the students that I interviewed for the reading survey. He is a shy boy when he is alone with an adult, but, when among peers, he is a lively child and student. He is one of the students impatiently whining that he wanted to read to the teacher. He is a very bright and excited learner who loves to be challenged. He kept asking for my help when students were completing their contraction activity. Each time I would go over to help him, he would ask me a question that he obviously knew the answer to. When I asked the same question in a different way, he quickly replied with the correct answer. He just wanted someone to pay attention to him and wanted to get praised for doing well. He is such a cutie; I couldn't help falling into his trap more than once.

Example Two. During my student teaching experience I interacted with all 23 students, but I found one student who seemed to need more direction and individual assistance. I decided to work more closely with this particular student, hoping to learn more about how to help him succeed. From the first day, John wanted to talk to me. He was constantly speaking in his mumbled way. I also knew that no matter what his teacher said or did he did not stay on task.

Example Three. I walked into the preschool classroom and was instantly pulled to Erin. She put her coat and book bag in her locker, and then she eagerly walked to the carpet and sat down in her special place. She was anticipating circle time. This amazed me because Erin used a walker to move around. She did not ask for assistance, and she was in her place ready for circle time before most of the other children in the class. I could tell in only a few moments that she was an amazing child.

In the following space describe a possibility for your case study and your rationale for selecting this particular student or situation.

Your responses:

____

____

____

____

Ethical Considerations

Next, before you proceed any further, you need to consider the ethical and privacy issues associated with your case study. Schools have become increasingly strict about protecting the privacy of their students. Federal legislation called the Family Education Rights and Privacy Act (FERPA) provides guidelines about who can have access to student records and when written permission is required to view records. Your school or district may have their own policies about student records and information that are stricter than the federal legislation, so it is important to inform your supervising teacher about your project, ask about student privacy and records policies, and obtain permission to conduct the case study.

In addition, the NEA has a code of ethics stating that individuals "shall not disclose information about students obtained in the course of professional service unless disclosure serves a compelling professional purpose or is required by law." This means, from a practical consideration, that you will code or change the name of the student, classroom, school, and district where the case study takes place to protect the privacy of your case study student. You will also not divulge information that might harm or invade the privacy of the case study student, which means, as tempting as it is to do so, you cannot chitchat about your case study with friends or family as it may cause harm or embarrassment to the student, the family, or the teacher. When you are in a school, even if you overhear other teachers discussing students in the faculty lounge, you should not join in the discussion. For some schools and groups of teachers it is the norm to openly discuss student problems and gossip about their families, but this is not an ethical practice. You may want to avoid the faculty lounge to keep from participating in those conversations. As an alternative, you can have lunch with the students—they will welcome your company, and you will get to know them better.

Describing the Case

Once you have selected and obtained permission for your case, you are ready to describe it. Thoroughly describing the case study is an important step leading to problem identification. Making observations, collecting data, and describing the situation will provide an excellent basis for identifying the problem. This is in contrast to the usual practice of rushing to problem solution without investigation or truly understanding the nature of the situation. The fact is, most of the time, teachers are compelled to act quickly to solve classroom and student problems without using a problem-solving process. They have so many problems and so little time that they are compelled to act in this unreflective manner. When writing case studies with my students who are experienced teachers, I caution them not to make an initial judgment about their cases even if the student has been in their classroom for a year. I insist that they wait until they have collected data and thoroughly described the situation before they propose a solution. Although at first they grumble because of the time this takes, later they are grateful for the opportunity to methodically investigate and solve a problem in a more satisfactory and professional manner.

Describing the case study means providing an objective description of the situation or the student. This clear, detailed, unbiased description captures the problem for the writer in order to prepare it for analysis. The more detailed and complete the description of the problem, the more likely that everything that needs to be considered during the problem-solving phase will be available for the writer's analysis. Following are two versions of a case study description. Be prepared to critique these.

Todd—Description One. Todd is a white male in the seventh grade. I am interested in him as the problem for my case study because Todd seldom completes any of his class assignments or homework, and as a result, he is barely passing most of his classes. Based on the few assignments Todd turns in and his answers to questions in class, Todd appears to have middle to high ability. According to his standardized test scores from the past 2 years, Todd is at or slightly above the mean in all subjects, except math, where he is at the 25th percentile. His grades in his cumulative file show a pattern of decrease in effort and achievement from elementary to middle school. His grades in primary school were all above average, but as he neared middle school they slowly declined. His sixth-grade teacher commented that Todd had difficulty staying on task and often didn't complete his homework. During English class I observed Todd as he read a short passage from the literature text (which he had to borrow from another student). He read haltingly, but he seemed to know most of the sight vocabulary, and when the teacher asked him a few comprehension questions, he appeared to understand the passage.

Observing Todd during the regular school day, I wondered why he seemed to have so little interest in schoolwork or grades. Todd seems capable of doing his work as long as the teacher is standing over him. If the teacher moves away, Todd will stop working and turn to other activities such as talking to his friends, fiddling with papers and pencils, reading a comic book, sleeping, or even on one occasion playing with a video game (the teacher took it away from him). Todd is rarely prepared for class. He often doesn't have his books, assignments, or even something to write with. He is also often tardy and has missed 10 days of school so far this term due to unexplained absences. He has been in ISD (in-school detention) for a total of 8 days as punishment for this and other minor classroom infractions.

According to the school counselor, Todd comes from a family that is struggling financially. Both of his parents work, but they have a large family and there have been recent problems with housing. The family lost the house they were living in and had to move to a small apartment. The counselor was concerned about how this change might erode Todd's already shaky motivation.

According to his homeroom teacher, both parents attended fall parent-teacher conference, where they expressed concern about

Todd's grades. Todd's mother explained that she had dropped out of high school in the tenth grade, and she was worried that Todd would follow the same path. The parents explained that it was difficult to wake Todd up in the morning, and they suspected that he skipped school by returning home after they leave for work. They were unaware of his absences. They were also unaware that he had been assigned detention. His parents were uncertain how to help him with his studies. His mother related that he usually claims he has no homework and that he seldom brings home schoolbooks.

While interviewing Todd, he seemed nervous and unsure of himself. He shrugged his shoulders at questions and rubbed his head. He claimed he liked school because he got to see his friends but said he is bored with the work and gets tired of listening to his teachers. He likes to stay up late to watch movies, play video games, or hang out with his friends, so he often feels tired at school and finds it hard to stay awake. He claims he would like to make better grades, but he doesn't know how to do that. He complained that his grades are so bad that it would be impossible to improve them, so why try.

Todd—Description Two. Todd is a white male in the seventh grade. I am interested in him as the problem for my case study because Todd seldom completes any of his class assignments or homework, and as a result, he is barely passing most of his classes. Based on the few assignments Todd turns in and his answers to questions in class, Todd appears to have middle to high ability. Watching him waste time in class every day I wonder why he has so little interest in schoolwork or grades. Todd seems capable of doing his work as long as the teacher is standing over him. If the teacher moves away, Todd will stop working and turn to other activities such as talking to his friends, fiddling with papers and pencils, reading a comic book, sleeping, or even on one occasion playing with a video game (his teacher took it away from him). Todd is a slacker and is rarely prepared for class. He is often missing his books, assignments, and even something to write with. He is also often tardy and has missed tons of days so far this term due to unexplained absences. He has been in detention for a total of 8 days as punishment for this and for all the times he acts up in class to get attention.

According to the school counselor, Todd comes from a family that is poor. Both of his parents work at low-paying jobs, and they have a huge number of kids. Recently they were thrown out of their house because they couldn't pay the rent. They had to move into a tiny apartment, and that must have made Todd really mad.

According to his homeroom teacher, both parents attended the fall parent-teacher conference, where they expressed concern about Todd's grades. My teacher told me that Todd's mother was a high school dropout and was worried that Todd would follow the same path. Todd's parents explained that he is really lazy and hard to wake up in the morning. They suspect he skips school by returning home after they leave for work and spends the day sleeping and messing around. They were unaware of his absences. They were also unaware that he had been assigned detention. In addition, they were uncertain how to help him with his studies. It seems pretty clear that they don't care much about their son and are not educated enough to help him with his studies. Parents like that never take care of their kids. They claim he says he has no homework, and because he seldom brings home his schoolbooks, they can't help him with his homework. These parents are not being responsible about their son's education, so it is no big surprise to me that he is failing in school.

When interviewing Todd, he seemed nervous and unsure of himself. His hands and clothes were dirty, and he is thin and unhealthy. I think he eats a lot of junk food. I saw him eating a Twinkie in the cafeteria the other day. I wonder if his parents have enough money to feed him. When I ask Todd questions, he shrugs his shoulders and rubs his head. I don't think he trusts adults because his parents have let him down so many times. He claims to like school because he gets to see his friends but says he is bored with the work and gets tired of listening to the teachers. I don't believe him about the friends, because everyone seems to dislike him. He says he likes to stay up late to watch movies, play video games, or hang out with his friends, so he often feels tired at school and finds it hard to stay awake. He claims he would like to make better grades, but he doesn't know how to do that. He complained that his grades are so bad that it would be impossible to improve them, so why try.

Critique of the Case Study Descriptions

What are your views about the two case study descriptions?

Your responses:

____

____

____

____

You will have certainly noticed the significant differences between the Todd One and Todd Two case study descriptions. While Todd Two is undoubtedly more entertaining, colorful, and gritty, the writer has broken every rule for writing a case study description. Todd Two is riddled with unprofessional ("slacker," "huge number of kids") and biased language ("Parents like that never take care of their kids."). Also, the language is unkind and disparaging of the subjects ("Recently they were thrown out of their house because they couldn't pay the rent."). If Todd and his parents read the case study description, I think they might feel hurt, embarrassed, and insulted. The writer also allowed gossip to creep into the description, including the comment the teacher made about Todd's mother and her education.

Todd Two also neglected to include data and other objective information that would serve to inform solutions to the problem. Rather than using data of test scores and information from records of Todd's educational history, the Todd Two description presents unfounded, premature, and inappropriate judgments about Todd and his parents ("I don't think he trusts adults because his parents have let him down so many times."): unfounded because the writer couldn't possibly make those determinations from the information presented, and inappropriate because they are unkind and unhelpful to Todd and his parents ("It seems pretty clear they don't care much about their son and are not educated enough to help him with his studies.").

Your case study description must be worded carefully not to use disparaging language. The tone should be clinical—"Just the facts, ma'am."

To counter all the admittedly exaggerated problems with Todd Two when describing your case, the writer should rely on objective data to the extent that it is available. Due to FERPA laws and district policy, you may be limited in the types of student data and documents you can obtain. Again, the writer will need permission for all requests for student data, to interview participants, and to administer additional tests and instruments. In my experience, the willingness of schools to provide access to student records varies considerably. Some districts will not allow a student teacher to review an IEP (Individual Educational Plan) for a special needs student they are teaching, whereas others will allow access to all records and permit student teachers to attend and participate in IEP meetings with parents and teachers.

A list of possible data sources follow. It is divided into three categories—observation, interview, and documents. No matter the type of data a teacher wants to collect, all data will fall into one of these categories. If possible, the writer should attempt to use sources from each of the three categories.

Observation

Instruments/forms/sheets

Running record/narrative

Commercial forms

Teacher made

Check sheets

Surveys and questionnaires

Open ended

Structured (multiple choice)

Likert scale (sometimes/always/never)

Audiotape/videotape/photographs

Interview

Individual

- Open ended
- Semistructured
- Structured
- Audiotape/transcription
- Videotape/transcription

Focus groups

- Open-ended/running record
- Semistructured
- Structured
- Audiotape/transcription
- Videotape/transcription

Subjects

- Student/subject
- Peers
- Current teachers
- Teachers from previous years
- Special education teachers
- Counselors/school psychologists
- Specialist teachers (coach, physical education, art, music)
- Principal
- Parents
- School nurse

Documents

Standardized test results

Diagnostic test results

IEP

Teacher-made assessments

Objective tests (multiple choice, true/false, matching, etc.)

Writing samples (rubric)

Reading tests (miscue analysis)

Performance tasks (rubric)

Portfolio (rubric)

Projects (science, art, drawing, etc.)

Oral presentation (rubric)

School records

Minutes of meetings

Attendance records

Detention records

Progress reports (report cards)

Classroom and school newsletters

Photographs

The list of sources for collecting student data is quite extensive and provides a variety of sources to select from for the investigation. Using an assortment of sources will produce a more detailed and comprehensive picture of the student or the situation. The data collection period of the case study process should be extensive, weeks long if possible. Once you begin to collect data, you may find the process surprisingly intriguing and motivating. Excellent teachers feel satisfaction as they solve and investigate classroom problems; it is the hallmark of an intellectual to be curious and to want to understand more about a situation.

Although a variety of sources is always desirable, excellent case studies can be conducted using simple data collection techniques, such as interviews with note taking, observations using running records, and collections of student work such as writing samples and typical classroom assignments. As a teacher, you will use what is available to you, what you have permission to use, and what is practical in terms of time. You may wish to conduct hours of audiotaped interviews of participants, but these are difficult to use unless you also have the time to transcribe them. I explain to classroom teachers that their data collection methods must be practical and within the realm of the duties of a classroom teacher. Teachers are not highly trained researchers or investigative journalists.

Remember, the data collection instruments you use must be appropriate for your case study participant. For example, if you want to administer a reading interest inventory to young children who often have limited reading ability, you must consider that factor. There are many inventories developed for young children that use pictures for responses rather than words. Instruments that have previously been tested for validity and reliability are described through sources such as the *Mental Measurements Yearbook* (Plake & Impara, 2001).

Interviews can provide important information and insight into student behavior. The evidence list includes typical participants that might be interviewed. Interviews can provide a more rounded picture of students by providing information about how they behave and perform in other settings. One question the teacher wants to answer first when investigating a student is whether the student has problems in other settings. This eliminates the possibility that the problem manifests itself in only one academic subject, classroom setting, or teacher. Parents and other caregivers can be helpful with history and how the student functions in other settings. Other teachers and specialist teachers bring their professional insight and experience to the problem. It is also important to interview the student you are investigating to see how they view the problem and their situation. Another somewhat risky but informative group to consult are the student's peers. You must be careful, because you don't want peers to tattle or "rat on" each other, but often a student's academic and motivation problems are related to social or self-esteem difficulties. Peers may be in a position to shed unique insight about how a student functions socially.

A dedicated student-centered science teacher in one of my classes was concerned about a young man in his class who was flunking science and seemed depressed. The student refused to talk with him. When asked, his friends confided that his father was in prison. The teacher called the young man's stepmother, who confirmed the student's account about prison. When the teacher asked how they could help the student the stepmother informed him that, with three children of her own, the teacher should feel lucky that she got the young man off to school on time.

For ethical reasons, it is necessary to inform the individuals you will interview about the purpose of investigation, the reason for the interview, how the information will be shared, and who will have access to the final project. You should also provide the results of the interview for their inspection and review.

While electronic media for taping interviews and observing student behavior can provide compelling evidence, parents and teachers may be particularly sensitive and resistant to their use. I have found that, while individuals may not allow me to use an audiotape during an interview, they will allow me to take notes. And while teachers and parents may not allow the videotaping of student behavior, they will allow running records taken during observations. Any use of videotape or photographs to be included in the final case study document will require permission from the school and parents. Most districts have strict polices about the use of student images.

Following are two examples of how student data can be reported in the case study description. One is very extensive and detailed. The other is less so, but both provide important information about the case study student.

Example One. Sissy is a 7-year-old second-grade African American student who attends a public school in ____ state. She lives with her mother, father, and sister in a middle-class neighborhood. Her parents both work outside the home and seem to be actively involved in their children's lives.

Upon examination of the student's earliest folder, no physical impairments were noted by her family physician. The Early Prevention of School Failure Diagnosis Test dated September 1999 indicated that the student scored moderately above age level on receptive language and visual memory; at expected age level on auditory, visual discrimination, and fine motor skills; and moderately below level on gross motor skills. The student took both the Otis-Lennon School Ability Test (OLSAT) and the Metropolitan 8 in October 1999. On the OLSAT, she scored 15 out of 30 on both the verbal and the nonverbal section. The Metropolitan 8 has three sections. The student scored 28 out of 40 on the sounds and print section, 15 out of 30 on the mathematics section, and 19 out of 30 on the language section.

The comment section of the first kindergarten progress report (after 9 weeks) noted that Sissy continually had trouble understanding and following directions. She had difficulty coloring within the lines, gluing neatly, tracing over lines, holding scissors appropriately (difficulty cutting on lines), drawing a person with six body parts, and tracing, copying, and drawing shapes. Her final progress report noted continued difficulties in these same areas. She still had problems following classroom and school rules, developing personal responsibility, and showing a positive attitude. Her final grades for first grade were a B in reading, Cs in writing and language arts, and Ds for mathematics and spelling, demonstrating a steady decline in effort. Her first-grade teacher noted that Sissy had developed a vision problem and had been given glasses to wear. She reported that her most vivid memory of the child was of her purposely breaking her glasses after refusing to wear them. When Sissy's parents were contacted, they showed concern but did not follow up with a replacement pair of glasses. Family Resources intervened, but their offer was politely refused. Currently in second grade, Sissy is still not wearing corrective glasses, though the need has been noted in her records.

Example Two. I observed Joe in my classroom from August 10, 2001, until December 6, 2001, for 1 1/2 hours per day. His locker is outside my room, where I also observed him. I made mental notes as well as written ones. I interviewed his Spanish teacher and spent about 30–40 minutes reviewing student records from Grades 1 through 10, again making notes.

Algebra I is taught in two semesters at my school. I have Joe for the second semester of Algebra I. He took the first semester of Algebra I twice before he passed it. Joe's grades for the first nine weeks in my class were 100, 71, 79, 97, and 100 for major tests. So far in the second nine weeks his grades are 56, 100, and 100. It is the norm that Joe does not do his textbook work. Even so, Joe is able to pay attention when we go over the work and does well on the graded assignments. Joe has impeccable handwriting and is quite meticulous—a good attribute for mathematics. During class, he is either asleep or an enthusiastic participant. On "sleep" days I have to call him down constantly for keeping his head on his desk. He argues back that he is paying attention. He spends a great deal of time helping others, but he gets distracted easily. He is very personable and social. He treats me like a "bud," and we often engage in conversations outside the realm of mathematics. He says he wants to be a lawyer.

If nothing else, Example One should give you an idea of how extensive is the data schools collect on students and fully establish that you never want to get off on the wrong foot with the kindergarten teacher. The Example Two description has less extensive student data and is written in a more informal style. Both are appropriate.

Observations of typical student behavior can be significant windows of insight into a student problem. Following are three examples taken using running records and journaling methods to demonstrate how compelling such data can be for understanding student and classroom problems.

Observation of Student One. I observed James during a morning skill-building activity. There were twelve questions on the board, and each student was also given a typed copy of the questions. James was sitting at his desk playing with his pencil and looking around. He was given a verbal cue to get busy, and he responded that he didn't know how to do it. The teacher told him to complete all the items that he could do by himself first, then ask for assistance. He said that he couldn't do any of them. When the teacher went over to him and asked him to read the first question to her, he did so. She then said, "OK, now what should you do to correct this sentence?" He responded correctly, and she continued to prompt him through the questions. She told him to continue with the rest of the questions. Shortly after she walked away, he saw me sitting at the back table. He came over to me and asked if I could help him. The questions asked students to name the oceans that border Antarctica. I asked him to read the next question and he did so with hesitation. I had to help him sound out several words in the question and locate Antarctica by matching the name on his sheet with the name on the map. He whined, saying that he wouldn't be able to find it because he couldn't read well enough. I explained that the continent map only had seven names and he could match what was on his paper to the map. Reluctantly, he approached the map at the front of the room. When he got there he just stood in front of it until one of his classmates came up and started looking at it too. He copied down the names of the oceans as his classmate was writing them (at least he saw where they were located on the map). When he completed this he went back to his desk and just stared at his paper. During the next 10 minutes he had to be redirected at least three times and asked the teacher to read something for him twice. After the observation was complete, I asked the teacher if this was typical for James. She indicated that, while he has the ability to do much of the assignments on his own, he usually tries to get people to help him rather than try to figure it out for himself. He often waits until the teacher goes over the answers with the class and writes the answers on the board before he completes his paper. She said that he can usually provide the answers orally, but does not want to write the answer down or read the questions himself. James is in my reading group for an hour each day where I see these same behaviors. He does not attempt to answer questions without a great deal of assistance and will usually not attempt to sound out unfamiliar words. He commented to me that he didn't want to write anything down before the class reviewed the answers because he would just have to erase it anyway.

Observation of Student Two. I observed Rosa during her spelling test and while the class worked on worksheets. Before the spelling test, Rosa put her sweater over her head to cover her hair. She moved the sweater off her ears so she could hear the words. She worked on the test with the sweater over her head and readjusted it every so often. She completed her test and raised her hand to have the teacher repeat a few words again. Finishing the test, the students began to work on worksheets as the teacher used the overhead. The children had a copy of the worksheet at their desk, and they were supposed to complete it as the teacher did the same on the overhead. While the teacher was at the overhead, Rosa was not paying attention. She was digging in her desk and cutting up pieces of paper. She kept her hands in the desk so the teacher does not see her. If the teacher looks in her direction, she acts like she is paying attention. The teacher finally notices what Rosa is doing and asks in a normal speaking voice, "What are you doing? Didn't I tell you that should be put away?" Rosa then puts the scissors and paper back in her desk. Later, during another worksheet, Rosa again was not following along on the overhead. She lounged across her chair backward and leaned on another child's desk. She was called upon to read a sentence, and she needs help with the word *cupcake*. The teacher breaks the word into syllables for her. Later, she drops her pencil on the floor. She climbs under her desk for a minute then comes up and talks with two other children instead of listening to the teacher going over the worksheet. The teacher then stops the lesson because the students are too loud.

Observation of Classroom. I was hired midyear to take a position at a school on an army base. The former teacher had found a position better suited to her. The class that I inherited was a second-grade class consisting of 19 students. These students were originally part of four different second-grade classes and were selected to complete a fifth class. My first impression was very alarming. The students were disruptive during classroom instruction and disorderly in the hallway. They were setting their own agenda in the classroom. Moreover, I knew I was in for a challenge when, on the first day, one of the students told me I looked mean and went on to say that if I was mean to him he would be mean to me. He further stated that he was not going to be treated unfairly. Soon after, on another occasion I told a student to finish his work. He told me, "No!" I said that I would tell his mother, and he said, "I don't care, call her. She won't do anything anyway." I realized that the class didn't care for me and they didn't want to comply with the rules I set for them. In one incident a student would repeatedly break my rule about sitting in their seats when I am teaching. I first warned her that she should sit down, but on the second offense I moved her card to punish her. She was angry and replied that she didn't like the rule, and she challenged me by asking why we had that rule. I reiterated that it helped to keep disruptions from occurring during lessons. She put down her head and refused to work the rest of the day. To be honest, I was not used to being challenged by a child and I was unsure how to respond. As the year went on, some days were good, where I could teach with only one argument breaking out. But overall the interruptions increased during instruction, with students tattling and arguing with each other. The students continued to display an overall disregard of the rules I tried to establish. Finally, I realized I had to try something different.

When another teacher observed this classroom, the teacher in the classroom observation was shocked into taking action by the alarming number of disruptions occurring during instruction. Often teachers conduct their own observations of student behavior by taking notes or keeping a journal of classroom events. If possible, it is helpful when a trusted colleague such as a counselor or special education teacher can observe classroom behavior while the teacher instructs. The observer is then free to take detailed notes, use an observation instrument, or simply count incidents of student behavior, providing a more detailed and accurate observation. Numbers and detailed observations are compelling evidence to illustrate a problem. Providing parents with a report that a student left his seat eight times during a single lesson is persuasive.

You are now ready to begin to collect data and write a description for the case that you have selected. On separate paper, write a one- to two-page description, including the sources for your data and the methods you used to interview participants and make observations. Don't forget to obtain permission and remember to leave judgments and conclusions out of your discussion until the next step, which is problem identification. It is important to refrain from identifying the problem during the description and data collection phase because you need to withhold judgment and avoid making premature conclusions until all of your data is assembled and ready for analysis.

Problem Identification

Once you have thoroughly described your case study, you are ready to identify the problem based on the evidence you have collected and the observations you have made. Although this may seem like a ridiculously obvious step, it is a critical one. It would be a waste of time, for example, to attempt to solve a nonexistent problem or pointless to remediate a student's misdiagnosed difficulties. Recall the Antonio Johnson case study from Chapter 2, where based on limited and informal evidence, unwarranted conclusions were drawn about the reasons for Antonio's lack of achievement. Consider also the Charlie Yazzie case study, also from Chapter 2. Charlie's teacher had developed suspicions and concerns about his achievement and behavior, but the teacher waited until he had collected data before he made the referral for a special education evaluation. The teacher wanted to rule out simpler, less drastic explanations before he went to the next level with his concerns. Even then the teacher did not make a diagnosis about Charlie. Usually such significant determinations are not made by classroom teachers but by special education teachers and physicians. But, as illustrated with the Charlie Yazzie case study, classroom teachers play an important role in providing evidence for assisting the diagnosis of student problems.

When you have gathered enough evidence, you are ready to identify the problem. Remember that a clear and obvious connection should be evident between the description and the problem statement. Recalling the Todd One case study description, following are two problem statements that address Todd's lack of achievement. Determine which would be more effective in identifying the problem and helping Todd.

> *Todd—Problem Statement One.* Todd faces several problems. His basic needs are not being met at home. Todd has developed work avoidance goals, lacks autonomy in his learning habits, and has poor self-esteem. Todd is in a world of his own where he plays and daydreams. He can do the work, but he chooses not to do so. He would rather move on to activities that take little effort and are more appealing to him. I have determined this by interviewing Todd, talking with other teachers, and observing him in class.

Todd—Problem Statement Two. Todd is deficient in some skills; however, one of his major obstacles is that he lacks the motivation to learn these skills. Todd is demonstrating "work avoidance" as related to the goals theory of student motivation. As Hauser-Cram (1999) explained in her article, some children are "mastery oriented" and will attempt to find solutions to learning problems. These mastery-oriented students are persistent when attempting a task or when trying to solve a problem. Todd is not like this. He gives up and does not challenge himself when he is faced with a task that does not come easy for him. He does not attempt to find strategies that will help him solve the problem but rather engages in other activities (talking, playing, drawing, or quitting). In addition, Hauser-Cram reported in her article that some children exhibit "learned helplessness" because they have not associated past academic encounters with positive experiences. They attribute their failure to internal things such as a lack of ability (I'm dumb so I won't be able to do it) rather than to a lack of learning and skills. This article also references how caregivers may affect a child's motivation to learn. According to the article, Todd may have developed learned helplessness behaviors because of the interactions he had with the adults in his life. If the focus was on being right or wrong, rather than discovery and persistence, Todd may have resorted to giving up rather than being wrong and displeasing those he loved. In addition, Brophy (1998) stated that students with failure syndrome (learned helplessness) fail needlessly because they fail to invest their best effort. Such students begin tasks halfheartedly and give up when they encounter even minor difficulty.

Which problem statement is more effective for helping Todd? State the reasons why you concluded this.

Your responses:

____

____

____

____

I suspect that you picked the second response, but let us examine why it is the better choice. Both problem statements explain why Todd is not achieving.

Review the discussion of Todd One to determine if the problem statements flow from and are logically connected to the description of Todd's difficulties in the classroom. Both problem statements describe a student who has academic ability but who does not persist in efforts to learn. They also state that Todd questions his ability to achieve and behaves helplessly and becomes disconnected from the educational process. The report documents that Todd has so little confidence in his abilities that he refuses to try unless the teacher is standing over him confirming that what he has done is correct. Both statements describe the same problem about Todd, but the second one cites research to support its claims. Problem Statement One asks the reader to accept the stated finding based on the conclusions and the limited experience of one person, the writer. Problem Statement Two supports similar assertions but uses evidence, research, experts, and motivation theory to defend a position. Which do you prefer to believe: the findings cited from the experience of a single individual or the collective experience of experts who have studied a field extensively? For these reasons it is extremely compelling and helpful to include research in your problem statement. It makes your finding more responsible and credible. The research can also lead the writer to the next step in the case study process, which is solution generation. On a separate sheet of paper, create a problem statement for your case study. It should be about a page or two in length and should include a specific description of your problem based on evidence from interviews, observations, and documents. The citation of research and theory is extremely helpful in supporting your findings.

Solution Generation

Once you have determined the problem, you are finally ready to determine solutions to solve the problem. Solution responses can range from teacher help to provide additional feedback and support for student learning to referrals made to psychiatric or social welfare agencies. I caution my own students not to select a student with the most overwhelmingly difficult situation. Many times those problems will go beyond the expertise of the classroom teacher. In those cases, the most helpful response a teacher can make is to recognize the problem and make a referral to the appropriate agency or source. The case you selected may not require such extreme resources and assistance. For problems that do fall in the realm of the classroom teacher's responsibilities, the more difficult and complex the problem the more collaboration will be required to solve the problem. A variety of professionals from the school and the community may be needed for collaboration to help a student, including special education, physical education, art, and music teachers. Also, others may need to be consulted, including school administration, librarians, counselors, nurses, physicians, social workers, physical therapists, occupational therapists, or even law enforcement officers. Hopefully, your proposed solution can be implemented in the classroom with the knowledge and support of a few school colleagues and the student's parents. Following are solutions that my students have developed to address their case study problems. These will provide examples of how various solutions can be written.

Solution One. I developed a plan to make sure that Erin is included in all the activities of the classroom. Using a walker shouldn't exclude her, and Erin is very determined and likes to do everything the other children do in class. When the children play "Duck, Duck, Goose" the instructional aide carries Erin around the circle so that she can participate in the game. When the children were playing a game in the classroom where they had to walk around in a circle, the aide held Erin's hand as she walked around the circle. When we are on the playground, I encourage Erin to climb on the playground equipment with the other children. She can crawl on the equipment and interact with the other children. Erin is able to play just like all the other children. She is determined to do this and I will help her.

Solution Two. With my concern about James's work avoidance and self-esteem issues, I think he would benefit by gaining self-confidence in his ability to complete classroom tasks. If James could acquire some of the skills that he lacks, this would help his self-confidence and his self-perception. Teaching skills that James has missed from lower grade levels would increase his confidence and allow him to take more chances when approaching a new task. I started working with James using a direct instruction reading program. This will provide him the basic phonic rules and strategies to improve word identification skills. We will work in the direct instruction program for 30 minutes each day, one-on-one. In addition to the reading instruction, we will spend 10 minutes each day on a program designed to increase reading skills by providing levels of reading (first words, then phrases, then sentences) on a timed basis. When the student successfully completes one sheet, they move to the next one. We will start on a level low enough to ensure success and then slowly move to more challenging levels. Many students enjoy this program because they can graph their own success and see immediate results. I will also provide James with high-interest, lower-level reading material so that he will not have to work so hard during his "pleasure reading" and be frustrated with its difficulty. James needs lots of practice reading. When James is working on assignments in the classroom, I will try and "chunk" his tasks (breaking his work into smaller assignments with short breaks between) so that he does not become frustrated with the amount of work he has to complete. Based on James's evaluation results—his verbal expression and oral comprehension—I believe that he possesses the ability to be successful. It will be my job to provide James with the necessary strategies and materials that will help him improve.

Solution Three. Maslow's hierarchy of needs theory seems to indicate Silvo's biggest problem. With both of his parents in jail and living with his elderly grandparents, his lower level needs of love, belonging, and esteem are not being met. He told me during our interview that he feels lonely and unwanted. Silvo feels inferior and is not confident in his abilities at school. To help motivate Silvo, I tried several techniques. I noticed that he did much better on drawing projects than on worksheets. Therefore, I gave Silvo autonomy or choice on certain assignments. Instead of a worksheet on a certain artist or art movement, Silvo can choose to create a drawing that illustrates that artist's style or the style of a movement. By giving students autonomy, their self-determination and self-esteem will increase (Anderman & Midgley, 1998). I have observed that, as Silvo successfully passes the visual assignments he chooses, his motivation and effort have increased in my class. Cooperative learning may also be helpful for Silvo. With his great artistic talent, I placed him in a group where he can help the other students with their drawings, and they can help him with his worksheets. In the group, he is no longer so isolated and the entire group will learn from each other. Cooperative learning improves student's behavior, relationships with peers, and motivation (Lyman & Foyle, 1988). I hope that this proves true with Silvo and that the success that he feels in sharing his skills and working in the group will raise his self-confidence and motivation and help him to make friends.

Notice how all three solutions provide a variety of very specific techniques and methods the teacher recommends to help the student. In addition to being specific, effective solutions are practical. That is, the techniques can be accomplished in a regular classroom. Solving complex student problems usually requires a number of solutions to address different aspects of the problem. Finally, the last solution provided cited research to support the techniques the teacher selected. Often, research that describes and explains the nature of an educational problem will also include methods to help remedy the problem. The solution flows naturally from the identified problem, which explains why solutions based on research can be particularly effective. The cause and the solution are logically connected. Often teachers in the press of attempting to quickly solve classroom problems will fling an entire barrage of solutions at a student problem, hoping, through trial and error, that one will work. This is an inefficient way to solve problems, particularly when answers could be provided by research that is as close as the library or the Internet.

In the following space, write several paragraphs that describe how to solve your case study problem, remembering to include practical solutions that address several aspects of the problem and using research as a reference to support your decision about how to best solve the problem.

Your responses:

Reflecting on the Solution

In the final stage of case study development, we will reflect on the solution. Although it might seem silly to reflect on the solution after conducting the entire case study investigation, this is a critical stage in the problem-solving process. It is here that the teacher decides if and how effective the solution was for solving the initial problem and for solving similar ones in the future. Is the writer, when they have implemented the solution, satisfied with the results? Did student learning increase? Was the classroom technique successful? Did student behavior improve to better support learning? Honestly answering these questions will serve as the staging point for the next time a problem presents itself.

It is also anticipated that the same problem or similar ones will surface in the future. If that is true, it is important to reflect on the generalizability of this case, its problem, and its solution for the future. Is it anticipated that the same or similar problem-solving methods could be used again, or will they need to be modified to produce different results? Remember, we utilized a problem-solving *system* to design the case study. We did not invest all of this time to simply solve *one* problem. It is important to determine if the system was effective and something you will be able to use in the future for most classroom problems. Good problem solvers review their efforts and the results to incorporate what they have learned for future reference. In the following space, consider what you learned, what you want to retain for the next time, and what you will change to improve your overall problem-solving strategy.

Your responses:

After developing an effective problem-solving system, you are now ready to dive into any pool or body of water and accomplish more than simply panting your way to the other side. Your new problem-solving system will keep you afloat and moving effectively for the rest of your teaching career.

REFERENCES

Anderman, L., & Midgley, C. (1998). *Motivation and middle school students.* (Report No. EDO-PS-98–5). ERIC Clearinghouse on Elementary and Early Childhood Education, Champaign, IL (ERIC Document Reproduction Service No. ED421281).

Brophy, J. (1998). *Motivating students to learn.* Boston: McGraw-Hill.

Hauser-Cram, P. (1999). I think I can, I think I can: Understanding and encouraging mastery motivation in young children. In K. M. Cauley, F. Lindner, & J. H. McMillan (Eds.), *Educational psychology* (pp. 151–155). Guilford, CT: McGraw-Hill/Dunshkin.

Lyman, L., & Foyle, H. (1988). *Cooperative learning strategies and children.* (Report No. EDO-PS-88–5). ERIC Clearinghouse on Elementary and Early Childhood Education, Urbana, IL (ERIC Document Reproduction Service No. ED306003).

Plake, B. S., & Impara, J. C. (2001). The fourteenth mental measurements yearbook. Lincoln: University of Nebraska Press.

INDEX

*Proper names in quotation marks indicate subjects of case studies

ABOUT THE AUTHOR

Renee W. Campoy, Ed.D., has a professional background as an elementary teacher and now as a university professor. She has completed extensive work with qualitative research methods and design and has also worked with alternative assessment and instructional methods with classroom teachers. She recently published a book, *A Case Study of a Professional Development School* (2000), as well as a chapter in *Effective Educational Partnerships* (2002). She has been published in the following journals: *Contemporary Education, The Professional Educator, Reading Improvement, American School Board Journal, SRATE Journal,* and *Kentucky ASCD Journal.*